Chronicles of Georgetown Life, 1865-1900

Other books by Mary Mitchell

A Walk in Georgetown (1966)
Annapolis Visit (1968)
Divided Town (1968)
Washington: A Portrait of a City (1972)
Glimpses of Georgetown, Past and Present (1983)

Chronicles of Georgetown Life
1865-1900

Mary Mitchell

Seven Locks Press
Cabin John, MD/Washington, DC

Copyright © 1986 by Mary Mitchell

Library of Congress Cataloging-in-Publication Data

Mitchell, Mary (Mary Atkinson)
   Chronicles of Georgetown Life, 1865-1900
     Bibliography: p.
     Includes index.
     1. Georgetown (Washington, D.C.)—History.
2. Washington (D.C.)—History. I. Title.
F202.G3M48   1986   975.3'03   86-15555
ISBN 0-932020-40-2
ISBN 0-932020-41-0 (pbk.)

First edition, October 1986

Design by Dan Thomas

Seven Locks Press
P.O. Box 27
Cabin John, MD 20818
(202) 362-4714

To Bill, my never-failing resource and support

A Prologue

My interest in Georgetown history was born of a happenstance. With a children's story in mind, in 1959 I asked Mathilde Williams, then curator of the Peabody Collection at the Georgetown Public Library, for local background material on the American Revolution. She said she could supply some, but that what was really needed was a book about Georgetown covering the period from 1860 to 1900. At the time of the Civil War, she noted, Georgetown was a Democratic enclave within a district administered by Republicans. The local population had come mostly from Maryland and Virginia and were largely southern in sympathy. But nobody had identified who they were, where they lived, or how the war affected them or the town itself. Only a single short unpublished set of reminiscences was at hand to illuminate this critical period. Miss Williams added that remarkably little existed about the rest of the century either.

Her challenge proved irresistible. Researching the Civil War period consumed seven years; writing it up and finding a publisher, another two. The result was *Divided Town* published in 1968 and now, alas, out of print. Miss Williams was pleased, and said her first gap was filled. Now, how about the second? Spurred by her encouragement, I set to work once more. The result is the volume at hand, representing another six years of research, and published originally, chapter by chapter, in *The Georgetowner*, during 1984 and 1985. Sad to say, Miss Williams, my inspiration, mentor and guide, is no longer here to advise and comment. She died in 1979, a great loss to the community. Fortunately, Robert Lyle, her successor, is a competent librarian with the same standards and knowledge of the Collection, and has been equally helpful.

While writing this book I became acutely aware of how confusing was the changing nature of Georgetown's relationship to Washington City. For the reader's benefit, therefore, I want to offer some clarifying exposition.

In 1751 Georgetown was a small Maryland settlement exporting tobacco when it received a charter from the General Assembly of Maryland as an independent jurisdiction. By 1789 its trade had become so active and the town so prosperous that the Assembly conferred on it the rank and dignity of an incorporated town. Soon thereafter, in 1790, it found itself part of the ten-mile square selected for the federal government's permanent seat. Assured that it would retain its separate self-governing identity within the District of Columbia, and anticipating economic benefits from the coming events, its merchants and town fathers were delighted to welcome the Congress in 1800 when it moved down from Philadelphia to the newly created capital city.

But presently, by 1803, the townsmen discerned flies in the ointment. Congress passed an Act depriving the two previously established jurisdictions in the federal district, Alexandria and Georgetown, of a vote in national elections. In addition they would have no representation in Congress. Georgetown's immediate reaction was an indignant petition to retrocede to Maryland. This was ignored. As time went on, its Councilmen discovered they could not build a bridge, levy taxes and print their own notes, dredge the harbor or, when the time came, introduce a railroad without an Act of Congress. In 1846 Alexandria petitioned for retrocession to Virginia, won it, and left the District. A green-eyed Georgetown watched as Alexandria's population increased and its economy improved.

Finding that its status as an independent municipality had become a farce, it tried five more times to achieve retrocession, always without success. Hostility grew with its neighbor across Rock Creek, the much newer City of Washington, even though the Civil War brought identical problems to both municipalities.

After the war major difficulties involving the administration of the entire District confronted the Federal Government. Finally in 1871 Congress passed the Territorial Act, repealing the separate charters of both Washington City and Georgetown, and setting up a single municipal government for the entire District. The Act did provide, however, that the old red brick town would still be known as the City of Georgetown and that its laws and ordinances would continue in force until repealed. Three years later, though, after the Board of Public Works had cut its shockingly expensive swathe through both Washington and Georgetown, the Territorial Act itself was repealed, and a tentative form of commission government was established.

In 1878 this form of government was formalized with the enactment of the Organic Act. Three commissioners appointed by the President would henceforth administer the District. The Act also established a fixed rate of federal contribution to the District's budget which, as far as Georgetown was concerned, was the best thing about it. Congress had at last realized that local taxpayers could not be expected to pay for maintaining the national capital city.

With the Organic Act—which remained the "constitution" of the District of Columbia until self-government was finally restored in 1975—, Georgetown lost its independence, though it retained its name and its status as a Port of Entry until a further Act of Congress, passed in 1895, swept away even these remnants of its legal identity. Nevertheless, despite being legislated out of existence, despite losing its economic self-sufficiency and its residential cachet, it continued to exist, and later flourish, as Washington's most distinctive and well-defined historic community.

Contents

      Prologue vii
I   Postbellum Paralysis 1
II Drums Along Rock Creek 6
III Survival of the Bobtail Bull 11
IV Henry D. Cooke: Part One 17
V Henry D. Cooke: Part Two 23
VI Takeover at Oak Hill: Part One 29
VII Takeover at Oak Hill: Part Two 35
VIII "The Impregnable Burg" 42
IX "Georgetown at a Standpoint" 47
X The Ludlow Patton 47
XI Newcomers—Male 60
XII Teapots on the Windowsills 65
XIII From Niederseebach to M Street 72
XIV "An Immense Vessel" 78
XV What's in a Name? 84
XVI Blacks in Residence 90
XVII After-hours in Georgetown in the 1890s: Part One 95
XVIII After-hours in Georgetown in the 1890s: Part Two 103
      Postscript 109
      Notes 111
      Bibliography 126
      Acknowledgments 129
      Index 131

Chronicles of Georgetown Life, 1865-1900

I

Postbellum Paralysis

In the months following the Civil War, an exhausted Georgetown struggled to regain its balance and cope with the anxieties of an era already impregnated with drastic change. After Abraham Lincoln's assassination none of the churches, not even Dumbarton Methodist Episcopal Church where Lincoln had worshipped several times, showed any public reaction to this event except the one least likely to do so. This was Christ Episcopal Church, a parish of southern sympathizers. With its facade draped in black, the church had tolled its bell for twelve long hours during the funeral services. The congregation's reaction was emotional. Caught up in grief over the defeat of the Confederate ideal, it mourned the loss of so many gallant young men and expressed anxiety about how the unknown quantity of Andrew Johnson's administration would handle the postbellum problems of the South.

The reaction of the Georgetown Corporation, the town's ruling body, on the other hand, was patently political and consistent with its usual independent attitude, war or no war, where Washington matters were concerned. After the assassination the Corporation appropriated a token $17.50 for "mourning goods" to drape the Town Hall, and only $75 for five hacks to drive the Mayor and a few officials into the capital to join the funeral cortege.[1]

But of course Georgetown was traditionally conservative and Democratic in its politics, and balked at cooperating with its neighbor across the creek about anything, not even in the immediate crisis of how to repair the bridge over Rock Creek at P Street. Called the Papermill Bridge ever since its construction at the site of a paper mill some sixty-five years earlier, it had burned down in 1826, and the popular crossing now was at Lyons' Mill site five hundred yards further north. Now the city engineers of Washington wanted to build a zigzag route down the steep embankments south of P, with pavements for two-way traffic each ten feet wide. The cost would be around $7300, Georgetown to bear half of it.[2] But the town authorities would have none of it, and continued to take the longer route into the capital. (Meanwhile, rival gangs of boys, one from Washington and one from Georgetown, fought at night with sticks and stones over possession of the deteriorating abutments to the bridge.[3]) It wasn't until 1871 that Georgetown surrendered, and then only because it had to when Congress passed the Territorial Act amalgamating the two cities.

Postbellum Paralysis

The Corporation's bitter hostility cut off its nose to spite its stubborn face. Most small tradesmen were in panic over how to reestablish trade with Virginia and find necessities like food and shelter for their families. Some had to sell their businesses to pay debts. Others who had been used to selling dry goods and clothing to the Virginia market and then returning across the river with dairy products and produce for the Georgetown market, now were unemployed. Still others tried a change of occupation. Barbers became dentists. Shoemakers became confectioners. A stoneyard owner set up a steamed oyster saloon, and felt the Lord blessed his wisdom. An upholsterer copied him with equal success.[4] The name of the postbellum game was a combination of enterprise, a cool head and adaptability. It was a trying, anguished period.

New construction here and there testified to a measure of wartime profits. At the west end of K Street, in the detached world of the waterfront, a weird latticework of new trestles, built during the war and stretching from the C&O Canal to the coal docks, let light through in patches onto a dusty stretch where stevedores and bargemen showed that here at least the noisy jarring rhythms of the wartime waterfront had not been interrupted. Coal, the product destined to save the economy, came down the Canal from Cumberland, Maryland, one hundred tons per boat, and was heaved onto the wharves. Hoping to catch the first coastal traders, Edward Linthicum, the wealthy hardware merchant living at The Oaks (Dumbarton Oaks), usually a cautious man, built a new wharf reaching two hundred feet out into the river. Two months later the jerry-built structure collapsed under the weight of seven hundred tons of coal.[5]

Substantial buildings in town and on The Heights also showed profits. Riley Shinn had added stables to his bottling factory on Olive Street. Members of the lumber companies' families had built new houses.[6] The energetic butcher clan, mostly German in origin and politically neutral, were riding high. Slaughterhouses, smokehouses, and blacksmith shops proliferated on The Heights both east and west of the Tenallytown Road. In fact, the District's assessor found a total of $166,270 worth of improvements had been added to Georgetown during this apparently stagnant period.[7] But these few signs of recovery were spotty and of little help in an economy of survival.

Overall, a sluggish, dismal atmosphere characterized the market place, usually the local nerve center, and indeed, the whole town. After the frenetic crowding of wartime, and the fulfilling sense of service felt by people who had nursed the wounded, the days of readjustment stretched ahead painfully empty. To make matters worse, sickness still threatened every corner of the town.

> "There is a great deal of sickness in Georgetown, more than ever before," wrote Henry D. Cooke to his brother Jay in Philadelphia, on July 8, 1865. "The air is tainted with the bad odors of camps, government corrals, bone factories and dead horses and mules.

Georgetown Life, 1865-1900

I fear scourge or plague. Low typhus fevers, diphtheria, etc. are very common, almost an epidemic. Everybody who can get away is going."[8]

Troops and lines of recruits might have disappeared. But wagons loaded with coffins, brought north up Chesapeake Bay, rumbled through Georgetown streets into Washington, and reminded everyone how recent was the bloody past. So many loafers, many on crutches, collected at street corners, chewing toothpicks, spitting, and hooting at ladies bound for church, that the *Georgetown Courier*'s editor said: "We need a public library, some place for them to go."[9]

Another aggravation was the numbers of livestock and unmuzzled dogs, some of them rabid, roaming the streets. Somehow the hogs snooping in the gutters were tolerable. They at least were dependable garbage disposals, and what would housewives do without them? But goats and cattle moved about freely too. Instead of taking the animal to the shed, the milkman had to take stool and pail to the cow. So many animals populated the scene the Corporation ordered everyone fined who kept his stable within two hundred feet of his house. Close as it was to a big city, pastures were still common in the rustic Georgetown of the late 60s.

The dreadful condition of the roads tying Georgetown to the outside world intensified its general sense of isolation. Throughout 1865 and 1866 moneys were appropriated to grade and repair the two roadways leading to Chain Bridge, Little Falls Road (MacArthur Boulevard) and New Cut Road (Reservoir Road). These roads did not actually lie within the town's boundary. But in 1858 Congress had given the Corporation jurisdiction over Chain Bridge traffic, provided it kept the Bridge toll-free and access to it in good shape.

At the intersection of these two main roads was the Drovers Rest Cattle Market and its many outlying pens. More important for many was its popular tavern. The largest of its kind in this part of the east, the market had been started in 1842, but had to close down when war began. A German immigrant took over the tavern and converted it into a bierstube popular with soldiers and travelers. Then, after an anxious post-war year waiting for the first droves of livestock to amble over Chain Bridge from Virginia, the butchers took over both tavern and market and held their first sale of 522 cattle and 940 sheep on August 25, 1866.[10] During the next year these sales were sporadic until the Virginia growers could redevelop their herds. But this first time, the old tavern must have rung to its rafters with the rough loud joy of drovers meeting with butchers and cattle brokers for the first time in five years.

The use of Georgetown's other link with Virginia, the Aqueduct Bridge, was a thornier problem. Merchants yearned for a free bridge so that goods and livestock could move into Washington via Georgetown, rather than over the Long Bridge from Alexandria. But because of the town's irksome relationship with the federal government, the merchant

Postbellum Paralysis

felt helpless. Ignoring their pleas for a railroad, the Reconstruction Congress gave control of the Aqueduct Bridge to the Alexandria Canal Company which wanted to divert the coal trade away from its longtime competitor and into Alexandria. The new owners, three Alexandria businessmen, were authorized to construct a highway toll bridge over the water-filled trough flowing with water from the C&O Canal.[11] The Georgetown merchants were so angry at this decision that they proclaimed it their duty to obstruct any efforts to repair the dilapidated basic structure so that they might gain help toward a railroad tie with Virginia.[12]

What everybody needed was a forum and outlet for popular grievance and resentment against the forces which seemed intent on destroying local fortunes. Fortunately, this gap was soon filled. In November 1865 the first issue of the *Georgetown Courier*, a four page weekly which lasted until May 1876, was published. This event probably had more to do with the recovery of civic pride and readjustment to postbellum change than any other in this critical decade.

In his thirtieth year and trained as a printer, John McGill, a cheerful and forceful, literate and indefatigable son of Erin, came down from Boston in 1859 to live in Georgetown and work as a Treasury clerk during the war.[13] Afterwards, he somehow found two newspaper presses and set them up on the second floor of a bookstore at 128 Bridge, or what is now approximately 3127 M Street. A small school for boys occupied the rear of the first floor. Some of them undoubtedly made pocket money as delivery boys for the thousand copies of the *Courier* published weekly, rain or shine, snow or mud. Georgetown had no job printer, so McGill filled this gap as well.

His publication resembled most other contemporary smalltown papers. The first page invariably ran a continued story dealing with love, jealousy, revenge—all the violent emotions—conveyed in the turgid, long-winded prose of such writers as Georgetown's own Emma E.D.N. Southworth. On the second page were international news and a forthright editorial projecting Georgetown's attitude toward any federal interference or action. On the third appeared local news and advertisements ranging from those for patent medicines through steamship schedules to real estate opportunities. A column called "Multum in Parvo" might supply gossip, recipes for baked custard, a sentimental poem by the town bard, Dr. William Shoemaker, and descriptions of a fashionable wedding. Catastrophe and disaster, such as the burial of Zeph English in his own corn bin for over two hours before he was dug out, almost dead from suffocation, brought out the best in McGill's sense of drama.[14]

A rash of freak accidents due to the current nervousness and jitters allowed him full opportunity to use his reportorial talent. Rebecca Tenney slipped on a cabbage leaf and broke her hip. A man and his Newfoundland dog fell through the sidewalk in front of Kengla's meat store into the butcher's ice-lined meat bin forty feet below and almost froze to death. An elderly gentleman out for his constitutional on Volta Place slipped on a marble shot by a little boy playing nearby. As he fell into the gutter, his cane whacked the backside of a hog snooping for garbage. The hog skedaddled for the nearest open doorway, which proved to be that of a carpenter working by candlelight. The candle fell off the shelf and all the shavings caught fire. The whole neighborhood was then treated to the awesome but exhilarating spectacle of the new fire steamer, the "Henry Addison," pulled by a snorting "Red Hot," the town's favorite firehorse, and his mate, roaring up the street accompanied by the volunteer force. The fire was quickly extinguished with water drawn from a spring which for once was of some practical use.[15] Its usual contribution was overflow from the pumphouse causing a morass of mud in the middle of this block.

Accidents like these were typical, and McGill in his seven-league boots managed to cover them all, often acting as intermediary or messenger boy to locate one of the town's thirteen physicians who were usually out on the street en route to a home-call. (In this period medical practice was not well organized. In 1870 only one of these men advertised office hours.) Later, when the steamroller of the Board of Public Works was tearing up Georgetown, and the neighborhoods were often closed off from each other entirely, it was even more evident what a valuable contribution McGill and his presses made to this small town trying to get back on its feet and convert an economy of survival into one of prosperity.

II

Drums Along Rock Creek

Among many postbellum anxieties, one in particular hung like Damocles' sword over each white Georgetowner's head. This was the imminent threat that Congress would enact the Negro Suffrage Bill, and there would be integration. During most of 1866 Congress debated the bill, which soon became a burning national issue. But in white Georgetown there was no issue. Everybody thought alike. Speaking for the whole, the Corporation declared: "The elective franchise to persons of color is wholly uncalled for, and an act of grievous oppression against which a helpless community can have no defense."[1] In a referendum three days after Christmas, 712 persons opposed the bill, and one supported it. (He was probably Charles D. Welch, a white man, who was elected mayor a year later supported by a large black vote.) The bill was enacted, Andrew Johnson's veto overridden, and by January 7, 1867 it became the law of the land.

Emancipation had given blacks the right to assemble in groups larger than six, a privilege denied them since 1795 by the Black Code.[2] The right to vote topped it, and the result was a kind of euphoria manifesting itself in ways the white population watched with a mounting sense of doom. Hundreds of blacks would gather from May to November in what is now Rose Park but was then called Jacob's Park, to sing and chant and participate in mass baptisms in Rock Creek, then a deep, healthy stream.[3] These gatherings whites could accept, but others were less tolerable. Almost nightly Negroes would gather in an old tavern house on the southwest corner of O and Wisconsin Avenue where a German immigrant rented a ballroom. "Both whites and Negroes patronized the place and kept up their howling and revelry all night, depriving those nearby of their much-needed rest."[4]

Black political activity was also extensive. Meetings were held in the new markethouse hall. Colored Progressive Republican clubs met at the Ebenezer Church on O Street for "disorganized and vociferous" assemblies, while mass rallies of the Grant-Colfax club were held on Rock Street, the south end of 27th Street. Complaints in the *Courier* of howling and shouting followed each meeting, and the neighborhood pleaded for some "abatement of the nuisance."

Most alarming to white citizens was the sight of blacks organized and drilling, armed not with wooden guns but with Enfield rifles and muskets.

Georgetown Life, 1865-1900

The Georgetown election—The Negro at the Ballot-Box.

The drilling was accompanied by "an incessant beating of drums along the Creek, one large and two small dogs barking, hogs grunting, little boys yelling, and so constantly that a truce is demanded by the bed-ridden, nervous and the enervated. Let it be done at the Papermill Bridge, for instance."[5] The usually patient John McGill, editor of the *Courier*, was also beginning to tear his hair.

If the neighborhood whites suffered nervous prostration, it must be remembered that for a long time Georgetowners had rejoiced in the comforting presence of Rock Creek as an effective barrier isolating them from Washington and allowing them to run their own show. Moreover, they had been accustomed to a certain deference and respect from Negroes. But an urban change of massive proportions had developed where the Creek proved no deterrent at all. No one knew what to expect from the new black people streaming into the town. Between 1860 and 1870 the black population of Georgetown increased from 1,935 to 3,271.

Emancipation had accelerated a great migration that started soon after the war began. As the Union Army advanced into Virginia, an ever-widening area was exposed to slaves wanting to enter free soil. Arriving in wagons covered like a prairie schooner, the refugees were found to be "the oddest groups imaginable: old darkies in wornout hunting jackets, ragged confederate uniforms, likely wenches in cast-off finery over homespun, babies in pink ruffs, funny creatures with wooly hair singed tawny red from the sun."[6] Was Freedom so sweet? asked the reporter. The further the armies went, the sweeter freedom became to these folk from the ravaged plantation country who, hungry, illiterate, fearful yet

Drums Along Rock Creek

excited, dragged themselves across the Potomac to the capital city expecting "Massa Linkum" to clothe, feed, and support them.

By 1864 an estimated thirty to forty thousand had come into the District and the Georgetown *City Directory* began showing new colored names by the dozen, 38 Johnsons in 1865, for example, compared to 10 found in 1860. The flow infiltrated every corner, with some people at one address one year and gone the next, and others replacing them in the same location.

The in-migrants came down the turnpikes, across Chain Bridge, then along Canal Road to Reservoir Road. Refugees from Montgomery County slogged along the east side of the Canal on well-worn livestock trails to augment the stream. Approaching Georgetown they would collapse on Callahan's Lot and Fenwick Hill. Today's Q Street had not been cut through, and here stretched vacant meadows bordered by 35th and 33rd Streets, the Presbyterian Cemetery on Volta Place and small private estates to the north.

Every neighborhood where urban Negroes had lived in the antebellum era now had to accommodate newcomers. On Volta Place where the Smallwoods and the Smackums had lived since the 1840's, a nucleus of 90 persons had doubled by 1870.[7] On O Street, across from St. John's Episcopal Church, ramshackle housing suddenly sprang up for 15 families. Below M Street on the west side of Thomas Jefferson Street and south of the Canal, a new segregation appeared. The west side became thick with blacks and faced a totally white settlement on the east. North of the Canal, whites inhabited both sides of the street.[8] Families squeezed themselves into every available nook and cranny, some settling in, others moving on. This floating population, drifting generally from west to east, would become a permanent feature of Georgetown life for the rest of the 19th century.

If the end of the rainbow for some was Washington, for many others it was Herring Hill in east Georgetown where free Negroes had developed a stable and self-sustaining community of 951 persons by 1860. Wisps of smoke from little cookfires in narrow backyards, pigpens, cowsheds, small two-story frame dwellings, barking dogs in the yard or roaming about; paths leading along a dirt road up to old Mt. Zion Church called "the Little Ark" on Mill Street, and beyond to the Methodist Cemetery, and across the footbridge to Lyons' Mill on Rock Creek; all combined to endow this compact region of fifteen blocks with the air of a close village community. In antebellum days, working hard within the strict regulation of the Black Code, a free Negro would set up a shanty, buy a horse and cart, and a year later would have a holding worth $100 to $300. Perhaps he had a wharf on Rock Creek and a shed where he would sell fish caught in the Creek or produce brought over from Virginia.[9] Many could read and write; some were hotel waiters and stewards, barbers and blacksmiths. But the majority were illiterate, and gave "common laborer" as occupation to the *City Directory* enumerator.

Georgetown Life, 1865-1900

Many refugees remained in Georgetown and became acclimatized because Georgetown offered them an atmosphere of agreeable coexistence far less biased then elsewhere in the south. This was true despite an apparent reluctance of the established black community to welcome these importunate strangers. Since this was an inarticulate population, its reaction is undocumented. It can be judged, however, by how few among the 250 families of Herring Hill took in refugees. Only five heads of household can be identified as giving them rearyard footage or shelter.

How did these new people earn a living, primarily the three or four dollars a month which was the going rate for houseroom?[10] If the tough and the strong could bypass the organized Irish gangs at the milling and coal end of K Street, they found ample opportunity. The flour mills were running again. Canalboats brought hay, grain and coal which then had to be unloaded and dumped into the holds of waiting cargo vessels in the coastal trade. Merchants, big and small, needed horse- and mule-drivers. A tannery at the corner of 30th and Olive Streets offered more jobs.

Then there was domestic, hotel, and tavern service. The Union Hotel had been redecorated into a "Pocket Tuileries," and new rooms added.[11] Lang's Hotel and Seminary Hotel, where several former generals refought the Rebellion daily over their common board, both needed help. Hundreds of Georgetown families had lost their servants and needed replacements. Over 500 newcomers found work this way, even boys of eight or nine who polished harness, blacked shoes, tended gardens, and chopped wood. But the existence of the vast majority was wretched and precarious. Unable to fend for themselves, many simply died; exactly how many is unknown. Constance McLaughlin Green in *The Secret City* said a figure for Washington was one out of three, and this probably held for Georgetown as well.[12] Despite this severe decimation, a comparison of colored names in city directories from 1864 through 1874 shows that about one-sixth of the in-migrants were still in Georgetown in 1874. (In 1872 enumerators began to stop designating color and by 1874 no designation was made at all.)

In November 1867 a rare firsthand glimpse of the newcomers emerges. Anxious to measure the dimensions of the educational task ahead, the Congress ordered the Metropolitan Police to take a census of the blacks in the District of Columbia. Twenty-four policemen were assigned to as many districts in Georgetown and set out with ledgers and pencils. It proved tough going. The *Evening Star*'s reporter wrote: "At one boardinghouse the officer got the names of each family member but not those of the boarders, getting answers like 'I'll give my name when I choose.' In the district bounded by N Street, Volta Place, 34th and Wisconsin Avenue, they balked at filling the blanks, saying 'I has nothing to do with that paper. You're not going to get me to my old massa. I'm a free darkie now.' After the census was concluded, Georgetown was found to have gained 1,349 blacks since 1860, of which 894 were children between the ages of six and seventeen."[13]

Drums Along Rock Creek

Confused as the picture was, the 1870 census reveals much about the newcomers and also about what emancipation had done for the oldtimers. Ten years before, there had been three mulattoes for one black. Now blacks predominated. Whereas Virginia had been a minority state of birth, its natives were now in the majority. In families older children of ten or over were reported born in Virginia, while the toddlers or babies were born in D.C., a gap of several years suggesting the disruption of the postbellum experience.

A surprising number showed initiative and talent which the slave environment had evidently stifled. The "common laborer" of 1865 was in 1870 a tanner, plasterer, cook, painter, butcher, cooper, or shoemaker. A "cartman" became a "reverend" and ministered the Gospel at the West Georgetown Methodist Church at the corner of 35th and Reservoir Road. Virginia produced more skills than Maryland—in particular, six carpenters who helped build Mount Zion United Methodist Church on 29th Street ten years later.

One result of the growth of Georgetown's black population was a mounting concern among white citizens for the education of their children—or at least their daughters—outside the public school system. On May 28, 1868, several leading businessmen and federal clerks assembled in the evening to discuss various solutions. Evincing a surprising sensitivity to the social and racial implications of their action, they argued about whether to go ahead with a private shool, admitting "they were pushing out the poor, and thus forcing the public schools to become pauper schools."[14]

Eventually, following the natural desire of parents anywhere to provide the best opportunities for their children, they founded a stock company with $20,000 capital to develop a plan to fill the gap caused by the loss of Miss English's Seminary which had closed in 1861 when it became a Union Hospital. Evidently, schooling for white boys didn't disturb this group, for there was no discussion about it at all.[15]

In the fall of 1868 Miss Sallie A. Lipscomb opened her boarding and day school for young ladies in the old Morsell house at 3108 P Street, a roomy dwelling with a spacious yard to the 31st Street corner. In a year or so the yard was sold, and she moved her institution to 3017 N Street. At length the stockholders settled her more permanently at 2900 Q Street in the antebellum John Dickson house where to the joy of families living in that neighborhood the Georgetown Seminary opened February 18, 1873.[16]

III

Survival of the Bobtail Bull

The passage of the Negro Suffrage Bill in 1868 served as fresh support for a bill to repeal the charters of Washington and Georgetown and govern the two cities as one under commissioners appointed by Congress. The idea was endorsed by George W. Riggs, William W. Corcoran, and Henry D. Cooke, who since his arrival in Georgetown in 1862 had become its leading citizen. As an alternative, the possibility of retrocession to Maryland again cropped up, for in the 1850s many prominent citizens had supported this.[1] But the Civil War intervened, and action was postponed.

But now, viewing the future with a jaundiced eye, the town fathers again considered retrocession. All had observed not only the decline of the waterfront but the rise of Washington's commercial importance, and they also recognized the grave threat of the Baltimore & Ohio Railroad in diverting trade away from the C&O Canal. With the increase in the Negro population, longtime citizens began to feel helpless. How could the town alone feed and house these poor people whose numbers increased every month? Congress wouldn't allow any railroad connections. Highways leading into Washington were becoming macadamized and smoothly rolled. Not so, those heading into Georgetown. Witness the Rockville Pike and Tenallytown Road; each was a muddy mess. Indeed, contacts with the outside were neglected here.[2] Exercised, angry and frustrated townsmen called a mass meeting at the new markethouse hall on March 5, 1870. Being stubborn Democrats in a world currently ruled by Reconstruction Republicans, they had strong opinions.

"Georgetown has a funded debt of $250,000 and no floating debts," cried one citizen. "THAT city's debt is over two million. Why should WE help it out?"... "It's a case of the Spider and the Fly. We have 18 men on the street. (He meant policemen.) We can govern ourselves..." "Washington wants Georgetown for building sites. Why, the Smithsonian building might have been put here...People here are law-abiding. We ought to stay separate." Judge James Dunlop took a practical attitude. "We pay 2/15ths of the county court's expenses, while our town's population comprises only 1/12th of the District. We ought to support annexation [to Maryland]." Then an oldtime orator, William H. Tenney, son of a shipping merchant from Salem, Mass., stood up. "Georgetown," he cried, "has no more chance of survival alone than a bobtail bull in flytime."[3]

Survival of the Bob-tail Bull

The discussion veered back and forth at fever pitch, without benefit of Robert's Rules of Order, which didn't come into use until 1873. Finally, exhausted, the crowd dispersed. It was still winter. There was no building, no trade. The merchants fretted and pulled their chins. Two weeks later the first boat at last came down from Cumberland with coal. This meant spring. What the *Evening Star* called old Fogeyism wore itself out, and busy once again, the business community tabled annexation for the time being.

Waterfront activity accelerated. The American Dredging Company from Philadelphia had worked a solid three months to clear out silt from the harbor.[4] Bituminous coal, mined in the Alleghenies and brought down the Canal to Georgetown where coastal vessels carried it to points north, south and east, was the new, felicitous element in the reinvigorating commerce. Weighing anchor at half-tide, drawing fourteen feet, the steamer *E.C. Knight* departed downriver with the largest freight load ever shipped out of the harbor.[5] The *Louisa Moore* of the New York Steamship Line brought four hundred cases of furniture for the Arlington Hotel being built by W. W. Corcoran in Washington, and returned to New York within thirty hours with apples from upstate Maryland.[6] Barks, brigs, and steamers of all sizes waited their turn at the wharves, and cranes to handle eighty-six waiting vessels were counted in September.[7]

John McGill of the *Courier* grew rhapsodic.

> The ring of Duvall's and Nicholson's many anvils in the iron works; the clatter of flouring and cornmills; the play of the hammer and adze in the cooper shops; the whirr and intermittent screech of saw and planing apparatus in Dyer's moulding machinery; moan of the bellows, and chink of the anvil in the iron shops, these and many other sounds of handicrafts can be heard everywhere.[8]

This reliance on muscle, the critical role still played by the Canal in the economy, the smallness of the diverse enterprises, their proximity to each other in a constricted hilly topography, all reveal how little Georgetown differed from other contemporary small towns in 1870.

The town itself, as distinct from the detached world of the waterfront, was taking on a new shine too. Everyone rejoiced that the economy was picking up, that those who had fought for the Confederacy were back in town and at work, that the multitude of new black people was being absorbed and finding work, thus making everyone happy to participate in the many small public events that enlivened daily life.

By the Canal the police showed off their plans for a new stationhouse with six waterclosets instead of the single castiron affair behind the entry used during wartime. Naively boasting they were do-it-yourself men, they described several false starts, such as how they had drawn a design which when measured didn't lead to the prison section and another which placed

Georgetown Life, 1865-1900

the backdoor on the edge of the Canal. Then a new fire engine, named the "Henry Addison" for the town's popular wartime mayor, arrived from Manchester, New Hampshire, and hundreds waited in line to inspect and admire this glittering specimen. Soon five serious fires in warehouses and mills provided a fortuitous chance to watch it in action drawn by "Red Hot," who had recovered from stepping on a nail and was in top form.[9]

The remodeled Union Hotel lent prestige to M Street. Sixteen Navajo Indians and some touring Japanese were among the first visitors.[10] Riley Shinn, who had sold his bottling business on Olive Street and bought the eighty-year old building, engaged Henry E. Searle, architect, to transform it into a "Pocket Tuileries" four stories high. To attract the gay and opulent Grant administration society, he added fifty more rooms, additional stabling for horses, and a women's entrance off 30th Street. Another attraction was a clubroom with national magazines laid about and a bar offering oysters from Morris Cove, New Jersey, with shells so thin you could see the bivalve within. Several retired army generals used it daily just like a London club. An ale vault and a polished marble stand dispensing Catawba wine completed these unique facilities. All were a credit to the town.[11]

For ladies, a greater joy sprang from the new drug stores mushrooming on convenient corners. Here they found patent medicines, fine French

Remodeled in the late 1860s to look like a "Pocket Tuileries," the old Union Hotel had lost some of its distinction by the time this photo was taken in 1917. Standing at the northeast corner of 30th and M Streets, it was torn down in 1936.

perfumes, braids, curls, and invisible wigs. Barbershops did such a thriving business that the Corporation had to legislate against working on Sunday. The police found one barber at midnight Saturday dyeing his customer's beard black, with one-half of it still red. The officer kindly allowed him to finish the job, but dragged him afterwards into the justice of the peace to pay his $5 fine.

Other recreational diversions opened up. Encouraged by the discovery that Negro suffrage had resulted in no violence and that the black newcomers were well-behaved and discreet, families hired more domestics. Housewives found they could leave home and trust their children to nurses living in. They took in entertainments at Forrest Hall, now over twenty years old, its prison cells from Civil War days removed and the space converted into an auditorium. People were thirsty for culture and diversion. Dr. Edgar Frisby, an English scientist, lectured on "Water and Its Elements." A noted Virginian doctor lectured on "Love, its Symptoms, Causes, Treatment, and Cure." Marie Nail, the smallest woman in the world, 22 years, 24 pounds, 27" high, was on exhibition. Mrs. Ann O'Neall held meetings of the Minerva Club where women with talent could sing and render a personal program, with refreshments afterwards.

Family excursions became very popular. Packing picnics, parents took their children to tournaments on Analostan (now Roosevelt) Island whose inspiration came from the South and which were modeled after those described in *Ivanhoe*. Young men dressed for jousting (despite 90-degree heat) in plumed helmet and carrying lances called themselves the "disinherited knights of the sword," and tilted at a ring to win a prize offered by a young lady dressed as the Queen of Love and Beauty. Beginning in October 1867, these tournaments proved so popular they were held for the next four years.[12]

Then there was the steamer *Wawaset* to Glymont, a riverside resort thirty miles south of Washington on the Maryland side of the Potomac. You could travel there in one hour and forty-six glorious minutes for a shad-bake.[13] Another favorite destination was Norfolk via the *Colt* whose brass and string band enhanced travel into Dixie, a peculiarly happy destination for this southern-sympathizing population. "What Ho," cried the *Courier*'s ebullient McGill, "Norfolk's corporate authorities intend doing the genteel thing. Is there one among you with soul so dead as not to go?"[14] There certainly was not. Trips were crowded almost to the danger-point.

One singular event proved that a chance to buy "antique" furniture is a timeless attraction. The old Poe mansion at the corner of Bank Street and Prospect Avenue was sold to a mailing contractor for $20,000, and a sale of its furniture brought $3,575. Formerly the Bank of Columbia, an honored institution of the Federal period, the building was once called "The White Cow" because when the Bank suspended payment in 1825, it had been milked so hard by its owners that it died.[15]

The local Tom Sawyers found recreation everywhere. Baseball had captivated masculine youth. Boys practiced throwing and catching at almost every corner, annoying and upsetting nervous old gentlemen who wondered where the police were. McGill gently chided the oldsters. "It is much more desirable for boys to be thus occupied than that they should be engaged in what is sinful, and be sent to the workhouse for some crime or misdemeanor."[16]

Another novelty was the velocipede, predecessor of a fad imported here after the Paris Exposition in the late 60s and soon to sweep the country. Nicknamed the "boneshaker," it had iron-rimmed wheels with a pedal on the front wheel. On December 10, 1868, the *Courier* boasted that Georgetown was way ahead of Washington in velocipedes seen on the street. In the spring a Velocipede Riding School opened on Wisconsin Avenue near M Street, with hours from 9 a.m. to 10 p.m. "One hour's practice was all that was necessary."[17]

Still another sign of the improving economy, more substantial than this composite picture of a growing sense of personal well-being, was the increase by 1870 in the number of new buildings, especially of new houses. In 1860 the census enumerator found 1,341 dwellings in Georgetown; but a decade later, 1,912. People were converting abandoned stables into dwellings and living in alleys, jerrybuilt additions to backbuildings such as ice- and smokehouses, and on second stories built upon sturdy wooden one-story dwellings. Many addresses in the 1870 *Directory* such as "near" or "rear," for whites as well as blacks, confirmed this practice.

Almost all the more substantial additions to the housing base carried no innovative or distinguishing earmarks. But their stout construction, as proven by their enduring and constant use in the ensuing century, demonstrated that Georgetown's cadre of master workmen, always one of its principal assets, had not been dissipated by the war's impact. This most fortunate circumstance also accounts for the hundreds of well-built dwellings erected later, between 1885 and 1900. The artisans, carpenters, plasterers, bricklayers, and painters living and working in Georgetown in the antebellum era had raised large families, including sons who evidently found their father's trade attractive enough to follow it, remain in Georgetown, and then introduce it to their own sons. In an era of tremendous change and demographic movement and commotion, these families did not scatter, nor did their households disperse. Their names appeared in city directories from 1860 through 1900. Son followed father in every case.[18]

The most spectacular, ambitious and altogether inspiriting building enterprise of this period was the construction by Henry D. Cooke between 1868 and 1873 on Q Street of eight first-class dwellings built as four twin villas. Known as Cooke Row, the new houses, as well as the decision of Cooke himself and his lively family to live in Georgetown, boosted the little town's self-image enormously. Representing as he did the money, success, and power of the Grant era, Cooke probably influenced the future destiny of Georgetown as no single resident has done before or since (with the exception of John F. Kennedy). Up to his time the only people to live

Survival of the Bob-tail Bull

in Georgetown and commute to Washington for the business day had been federal clerks. Cooke was the first big-time businessman to follow the commuter's life-style, albeit in his horse-and-carriage. Introduced to this agreeable pattern, many later settled here to follow his example. The ripple-effect gradually shifted the local business focus into real estate where Cooke became the catalytic factor. As such, he deserves two chapters to himself.

IV

Henry D. Cooke
Part One

Next time you pass Downing & Vaux House at the intersection of Q and Thirtieth Streets, where 1537 30th Street stands today, wing a thought up to Oak Hill Cemetery where Henry David Cooke lies buried in patriarchal aplomb on Reno Hill amid twenty-one children and grandchildren. Famed for his personality and panache, his accomplishments, and his vision for Georgetown, Cooke was Georgetown's first big-time commuter. His presence attracted other men of his social and economic stamp to move to Georgetown and to settle in substantial and handsome Victorian dwellings.

The apogee of Cooke's unusually active career came when President Ulysses S. Grant appointed him Governor of the new Territory of the District of Columbia in 1871. Jay, Henry's sounder, more successful brother, the financier of the Union Army, was an even better friend of President Grant's than was Henry. He had wanted Henry to have this political plum to add lustre to the family banking house in Philadelphia, Jay Cooke & Co.

When Henry first arrived in Washington in March 1861 for Abraham Lincoln's inauguration, he had had unusually wide experience for those days. Born in 1825 in Sandusky, Ohio, he was the son of Eleutheros Cooke, one of the earliest easterners to settle west of the Appalachians and a Republican congressman from Ohio in 1831-1832. Cooke graduated at twenty from Transylvania University, the forerunner of the University of Kentucky at Lexington.[1] Contracting the wanderlust, he had himself posted to Valparaiso, Chile, as attaché to the American Consul. But California soon beckoned, and he left Chile to engage in profitable shipping enterprises up and down the Pacific Coast. Clever and intelligent, he also learned navigation; when the captain died on one ship plying between Cape Horn and San Francisco, Cooke navigated the vessel safely back to her home berth. Although he made a sizeable fortune, it was wiped out in a San Francisco fire, and he returned east in 1849.[2]

Somehow he found time to court his future wife Laura, born in 1830 in Utica, New York. Married in 1849, they first lived in Philadelphia, where Henry handled the financial department of the *United States Gazette* and Laura produced two children. With this new responsibility, he abandoned the roving life, and the family settled in Columbus, Ohio, where Cooke served as editor of the *Ohio State Journal*, state organ of the Republican

Henry D. Cooke—Part One

Henry D. Cooke

party, for the rest of the decade. Here he strongly backed Salmon P. Chase, then governor of Ohio, and the two men became such intimate friends that Chase named Cooke executor of his will and was buried in Cooke's lot at Oak Hill Cemetery in Georgetown upon his death in 1873. His body remained there until the Chase family moved it to Ohio in 1886.[3]

When Lincoln formed his cabinet, Chase became Secretary of the Treasury, and Jay Cooke persuaded Henry to move to Washington and become a special Treasury agent selling war bonds. Even though Henry had fumbled the business end of things while with the *Ohio State Journal*, and had contracted large debts (which Jay underwrote),[4] he was skilled in public relations and in lobbying. In February 1862 Jay Cooke & Co. opened an office at 452 15th Street opposite the Treasury building. Needing his brother's skills, Jay then set him up as president of the First National Bank of Washington, chartered on July 16, 1863, with a capitalization of $500,000.

In the spring of 1862, when they moved to Washington, Henry and Laura did a surprising thing. At a time when the fashionable area in Washington centered around Lafayette Square, Henry and Laura chose Georgetown. When they actually moved to the house on 30th Street—then known as 1517—is unclear. But they were certainly on their front verandah looking west when the second Battle of Bull Run took place on the sultry weekend of August 30, 1862, for Henry wrote Jay how "distinctly the cannonading and even the long volleys of musketry could be heard."[5]

The Cookes' first acquaintance with the old red brick town came about through a business deal Henry and Jay had undertaken. They piloted a law through Congress authorizing the construction of the first street railroad in the District, called the Washington & Georgetown Street Railroad. It consisted of a line of horse-drawn omnibuses running between the Navy Yard and the home barns in a former tobacco warehouse on M Street where Georgetown Park shopping mall stands today. Henry presided over the formal opening of the line on November 15, 1862.[6]

By that time he and his family were residing in the elaborate Italianate villa at 1517 30th Street with their one thousand ounces of silver plate, four watches, a large oil portrait of Eleutheros Cooke, many crates of

Georgetown Life, 1865-1900

books, and two carriages, personal possessions which the D.C. Assessor for wartime property taxes found worth $3,200.[7] The house had been built by Francis Dodge, Jr., in 1850-1852. But following the bankruptcy of F. & A.H. Dodge, the export-import shipping firm, in 1857, Francis and his family had moved out to live with his wife's family, and the house had gone into the hands of the receiver who, conveniently, was his sister, Mrs. Mary Marbury. When Cooke came along, she moved to 3052 P Street, and rented him the place until financial arrangements could be completed and the deed of purchase recorded on April 1, 1864. The Cookes paid $25,000, double the assessed value of the house in 1860. The title was in Laura's name.[8]

Why did the Cookes choose modest, unpretentious Georgetown? Having just taken over a major business in the town, he may have felt obligated to live there. But an equally significant reason was the alluring contrast between the small, settled little town with its long tradition, its hilly topography and its southern established society, and raw, flat Ohio still growing out of its frontier phase. Or perhaps Laura made the decision for the same reason that prompted Mrs. Newton D. Baker, wife of the Secretary of War in Woodrow Wilson's cabinet, to select 3017 N Street for her family in the quiet, unfashionable Georgetown of 1917. Across the open space that passed for Q Street in 1862, two large estates, open, wild and uncultivated, ran north up the hillsides to The Heights. The Cooke's children were twelve, nine, six, four and one, and like Mrs. Baker, Laura must have wanted room for them to play and enjoy the countryside.

The house Henry moved into, in 1862

19

Henry D. Cooke—Part One

A church affiliation was another important decision. Instead of joining Christ Episcopal Church two blocks away, whose communicants were southern sympathizers and mostly of southern extraction, the family chose St. John's Episcopal Church on O Street with its more heterogeneous and definitely more northern congregation. They made this selection even though it meant crossing Wisconsin Avenue, as much of a deterrent then as it is today, even in a horse-drawn carriage.

In the late 1860s, even though president of Washington's largest bank, Cooke either didn't have enough to challenge him or felt he needed more of a stake in his adopted hometown. He liked projects, and having found the Andrew Johnson administration incompatible for his energies, he turned to real estate. In that era a country estate had become the status symbol of a successful businessman, and his brother Jay's showplace near Philadelphia named "Ogontz" embodied this concept. Wanting to emulate him, in May 1866 Henry offered Mrs. Margaret Barber $50,000 for her Italian villa north of Georgetown on a hilltop. But Mrs. Barber, a longtime widow who had lost four of her five children to scarlet fever in one awful month twenty years earlier, had for years enjoyed opening up her 62-acre estate and its woods to church and children's picnics. So, feeling her place was worth a lot more anyway, she turned Cooke down.[9] (In 1881 she sold it to the U.S. Navy for its Naval Observatory for $72,000.)[10]

Cooke then turned his energies back to his own residence at 1517 30th Street. Calvert Vaux and Andrew Jackson Downing had designed the original structure in 1850. Though Downing died in 1852, Vaux was still building his famous cottage villas in Philadelphia. But ignoring Vaux, Cooke engaged another Philadelphia architect, Thomas B. Plowman, to design a three-story addition measuring 30' x 50' on each floor. A local contractor, Joseph F. Collins, was in charge of building the addition, and the plumbers, gasfitters, and painters were local too.

> The first story is to be used for a library and music room, the second for bed chambers and third for a billiard room. The old part is being remodelled. The whole interior will be frescoed by K. Kaiser, of Philadelphia. Handsome verandahs and bay-windows are being added to the front and back of the building. The exterior will be finished in imitation of brownstone, and the blinds painted a French green. Upon the roof will be a cupola, elevated as to give a fine view of the two cities, Arlington Heights, and the Potomac River. The residence and grounds will be surrounded by a handsome iron fence with a granite base.[11]

In the new library we can imagine Laura and Henry opening the crates of books brought from Ohio and arranging the sets of Washington Irving, James Fenimore Cooper and Sir Walter Scott, making it into the kind of library a gentleman of that era was supposed to own and display. The most valuable book, an edition of *Paradise Lost* illustrated by Gustave Doré,

Georgetown Life, 1865-1900

The house at 1517 30th Street with the three-story addition Henry made in 1867.

was placed on a prominent table. In the dining room hung the oil portrait of Eleutheros Cooke.[12] To staff the enlarged mansion, Laura required one Irish servant, a maid from Prussia, and four black servants, including a coachman. A French governess, thirty years old, had come with the children from Ohio.[13]

Still more elaborate trappings were found necessary. Keeping a private carriage and your own horses at home was much more of a luxury then than keeping a car today. You had to have a groom, a coachman, a storage space for hay and oats, and wall-space to hang harness and tack. So most Georgetowners kept their horse and gig in a convenient livery-stable, of which Georgetown had five in 1867.[14] It is no wonder, therefore, that the reporter from the *Daily Constitutional Union* in his description of the Cooke's opulent establishment should devote a paragraph to the new stable:

> Mr. Cooke has had erected a short distance from his house, a model coachhouse and stable. To see this alone is worth a visit to the premises. It is built of brick, and is two stories high, painted and penciled on the outside; and the inside walls are finished in imitation of blue granite, and the woodwork finely grained.[15]

But Cooke had even grander plans. Cattycorner from his mansion lay eight unimproved acres extending from Q to R. Streets. With money burning in his fingers and creative energy in his mind, Cooke envisioned erecting a fashionable row of villas on this property. On July 9, 1867, he purchased it "for the sake and benefit of Laura S. H. Cooke"; again; title was in her name.[16]

Considering his active, aggressive nature, this project must have held high excitement for him. In 1842 Martha Parke Custis Peter, who had built Tudor Place, had received from the Georgetown Corporation its consent to keep Stoddert Street (as Q was called) closed. Already in 1866 Cooke had approached the Corporation for permission to "open, grade, curb, and gutter" Q Street from 28th Street west to Wisconsin Avenue. Evidently, his proposal was given the green light, for by June 14, 1867, the formidable earth-moving operation was accomplished, although only through to 31st Street. (It wasn't until 1913 that Q was cut through to Wisconsin Avenue.)[17]

The stage was now set for building Cooke Row.

V

Henry D. Cooke
Part Two

Cooke Row was probably planned in the late summer of 1867 with Joseph Collins, the local contractor who lived at 3016 O Street. Consultants were Starkweather & Plowman who were described by the *Evening Star* of June 30, 1868 as "accomplished architects, engineers and surveyors of Washington." Each house was to cost $17,000.[1]

Until that time most Georgetown houses of any consequence had been built with several backbuildings, such as a small stable, an outhouse, a smokehouse, an icehouse, and miscellaneous sheds for chickens, tools, wagons, etc. But Cooke stipulated that the four double-villas he was planning were to have none of these, that all facilities were to be incorporated in the house-plan, and that the single outbuilding would be a party-stable, straddling the property line. Each lot was 43 by 140 feet deep with a sizeable backyard. It was typical of Cooke that the villas' dimensions proved too generous to accommodate the stable, which thereupon was summarily eliminated.

Whether the rooflines, French attic on Nos. 1, 2, 7 and 8, and Italianate Gothic on Nos. 3, 4, 5 and 6, were originally planned that way is unclear. Cooke was about to take his family abroad to visit the 1867 Paris Exposition. Certainly on his return in the spring of 1868, he was full of the latest French architectural designs featuring the Mansard roof. When pierced with dormers, a Mansard provided a more spacious, economical attic story than the Italianate design, so popular in the antebellum era. The architectural mix remains a puzzle, however; perhaps Cooke simply wanted to give buyers a choice of two styles.

When the Cookes returned from Europe, they decided to cancel another project initiated by Laura. The previous summer she had planned a large mansion of Seneca stone on the property on The Heights opposite Oak Hill Cemetery's gatehouse, and had ordered the land cleared.[2] This was to provide a distraction from the grief of losing little Lizzie who had died at six months and was buried at Oak Hill, on April 18, 1867.[3] But still mourning her little Lizzie, she evidently could not face being so near the Cemetery, and so canceled the building project. In any case, plenty of distraction was available from their front verandah on 30th Street as Collins's brickmasons began raising the walls of the four double-villas.

After the election of Ulysses S. Grant as president in 1868, Cooke quickly became one of Washington's outstanding figures and had no trouble

Henry D. Cooke—Part Two

A reception for President Ulysses S. Grant
(Library of Congress, Prints and Photographs Divisions)

with the Georgetown Corporation when it came to executing street repairs in his neighborhood. In August 1870 he could be seen on his corner observing the repairs to 30th Street from N north to Q. "The road was dug up twelve inches, then gravelled, and earth from Red Hill [Mount Alto where the Russian Embassy is today] laid down in alternate layers, each layer made smooth by rolling the stone between two horses, so that drivers could take either side as well as the centre, and four carriages go abreast."[4]

Considering his numerous public associations, it is no wonder he wanted his own house to be easily accessible. By 1871 he was an officer on sixteen boards and committees in Washington, more than any other public figure in private life.[5] (Alexander R. Shepherd was on fifteen.) His name appeared often in the press. On May 28, 1869, for example, it was reported that he entertained the board of William W. Corcoran's Gallery of Art at its first official meeting, and followed this with a formal dinner the same evening at his mansion on 30th Street for President Grant and his cabinet. He took the press on pleasant excursions to Glymont during which, typically expansive and unrealistic, he rhapsodized about Georgetown's future, predicting a population of one hundred thousand within two decades compared to the ten to fifteen thousand then present.[6] That same year he even succeeded in persuading the Georgetown Corporation to cooperate with the Washington City Council in building the new bridge over P Street at Rock Creek, no mean feat with this stubborn body.[7]

Meanwhile Congress began considering the creation of a territorial

Georgetown Life, 1865-1900

Cooke Row (in 1985)

government for the District of Columbia which would amalgamate the cities of Washington and Georgetown and provide a Governor appointed by the President and an elected mayor for each city. Although a commission form of government was also considered, eventually, on February 21, 1871, Congress enacted the Territorial Act. President Grant appointed Cooke as Governor and also named a legislative council of eleven members. The charters of the two jurisdictions were to remain in force until June 1, so that the Corporations could collect moneys owed, redeem notes, and meet claims. After that date they would lose their charters. The reaction of Georgetowners was incredibly passive. After all the growls, the only regret which that indefatigable listening post at the *Courier*, John McGill, could pick up was that "now the endeared name of Henry D. Cooke would be lost in the austere title of Governor."[8]

Another vital part of the Act provided for a Board of Public Works. After the battering the capital city had endured in wartime, its roads, public buildings, and physical appearance had deteriorated, and once more it had assumed the aspect of a sleepy southern town, with livestock wandering about at will, even into Senators' houses. Businessmen and the Board of Trade, alarmed by agitation to remove the capital to St. Louis, supported immediate public improvements, despite the desperate financial straits of the Washington budget. Cooke's friend, Alexander R. Shepherd, was appointed head of this new Board.

On May 15, following the inauguration of the new legislature, all District Republican clubs, the Fire Departments, and other militia formed

Henry D. Cooke—Part Two

a torchlight parade to march along Pennsylvania Avenue past the White House through excited throngs to the residence of the new Governor. The old town had never been much given to attempts at formal grandeur on festive occasions. But now its townsmen festooned Cooke's mansion with flags and bunting and illuminated his verandahs and fence-rails. With Shepherd and others beside him, Cooke received the honors as the band struck up "Hail to the Chief!"

Cooke said only a few words, pleading indisposition. His diffidence was out of character, and three reasons may account for it. In the first place, the Cookes' youngest son Guy, only six months old, had died and been buried beside little Lizzie on March 6. (His death was such a blow to the Cookes that Matthew Brady was commissioned to craft a porcelain image of the boy's head.[9] In addition, the Cookes bought a baptismal font and had it engraved with Guy's name before giving it to St. John's Episcopal Church on O Street.)

A second reason may indeed have been Henry's own health. He was to die ten years later, at the premature age of fifty-six, of Bright's Disease. Always a man to burn his candle at both ends, he may have been subject to temporary physical weakness related to this incipient condition.

A third and more likely reason was his realization of what the loss of their traditional independence would mean to the proud Georgetowners. The Corporation's books had been in the black, and in such good shape that leading townsmen growled frequently about helping out "that neighbor across the Creek." Some hoped that Cooke might now lobby effectively for the introduction of a railroad. If he did try, no results came of his effort. Later, when the Board of Public Works was in town, however, he did see to it that none of the local contractors lost business to Washington jobbers. Practically all the big assignments went to local pavers, stoneyards, and lumberyards. At one point he even stepped in personally to settle a stevedores' strike when the workmen wanted $2 per day instead of the current $1.50, and saw that they got their raise.[10]

By this time other improvements resulting from the Territorial Act were obvious. All "town rabbits" and "cholera-breeders," i.e., hogs, had been consigned to the obscurity of sty and stable. Lime had been spread on the more infectious streets, and alleys cleaned up. Moreover, and this applied to a man's pocketbook, most notes of the former Georgetown Corporation had been redeemed, even some as small as $5.[11] After all, it would be foolish to look such gift horses in the mouth, and Cooke's popularity and residence in Georgetown did much to tone down hostility and resentment. The carping locals accepted the loss of jurisdiction with at least superficial equanimity, agreeing that it was "not practicable to keep separate accounts, and observe separate laws. The arrangements have the merit of greater simplicity."[12] Since the laws involved such matters as which streets funeral processions could use and where drovers moved their livestock through town en route to Drovers Rest, uniformity did seem practical.

Georgetown Life, 1865-1900

Henry and Laura now rejoiced in his new post. She received Tuesday afternoons between two and four, and her receptions proved so popular that in January 1873 the hours were extended to five o'clock. At one evening reception and ball on Washington's Birthday, one thousand people, including President and Mrs. Grant, attended. To gain entrance, the line of carriages on 30th Street was so dense an hour's wait was necessary. Once inside, the gay and opulent Italianate villa was atwitter with the songs of hundred of canaries. This, combined with the stunning arrangement of japonicas, azaleas, date palms, acacias and other rare plants from local greenhouses, created a lovely setting for the twirling, bustled gowns during waltz time.

The year 1873 was noteworthy also because of the wedding on June 7 of Henry D. Cooke, Jr., to Anna Howell Dodge, daughter of A. H. Dodge who lived at 2819 P Street. Wedding presents valued at $30,000 were excelled only by the gift from Laura and Henry of a house and lot, No. 5 Cooke Row (today's 3019 Q Street), the only one with a castiron spike topping the rooftop gazebo and the first villa in the Row to have a bona fide owner.[13]

The Cookes could not foresee how providential this gift was. On September 18, 1873, Jay Cooke & Co. declared bankruptcy, and at 12:15 p.m. closed its doors in Philadelphia. Jay asked Henry to resign his office as Governor, which the latter did reluctantly.[14] Records are unclear as to Henry's title to his house. But we can assume that the bank held the mortgage on it, and that when Jay Cooke & Co. declared bankruptcy, it went into the hands of the receiver. Henry and Laura with their three remaining children, governess and two servants then moved in with the young couple at No. 5 Cooke Row. By the fall of 1874, though, the Cookes were to be found at Villa No. 1, 3007 Q Street, which became their permanent home. The sets of American classics again lined their library shelves and, appropriately, *Paradise Lost* was again out on the table. If Cooke didn't have the space or grandeur to which he was accustomed, at least he had around him all the familiar trappings.[15]

If he was depressed by the sight of his former house cattycorner across the street, endowed as it was with so many happy associations, no evidence at hand can prove it. Indeed, it was not in Henry's nature to brood. Subsequent activities suggest that he considered bankruptcy only a temporary hindrance and shrinking his lifestyle a challenge rather than an indignity. Entering some Colorado mining ventures and capitalizing on the recuperation of the Northern Pacific Railroad, he soon began to regain his former affluence.[16]

Another responsibility promoted his reputation. Salmon P. Chase, who had served as Secretary of the Treasury in Lincoln's cabinet and later as Chief Justice of the United States, had named Cooke executor of his will. (He had died in New York City May 7, 1873.) After two years of litigation and appraisals had been taken care of, it was time to sell the statesman's effects. The sale took place April 27, 1875, and Cooke made all the arrangements. Held at Edgewood, Chase's large estate near Glenwood

Henry D. Cooke—Part Two

Cemetery, it offered all manner of first class items, from blooded horses, fine carriages and beautiful mirrors to one thousand yards of Brussels carpet and an arm-chair presented to Chase by the former Massachusetts senator, Charles Sumner. A superb library constituted a major attraction. Cooke arranged for omnibuses to take interested buyers out to Edgewood and to return them after the sale.[17] When the sale was completed, he took his family to Europe in June and, on return, up north to a cooler climate for the rest of the summer.[18] Going bankrupt in Henry Cooke's style seemed to entail no hardship at all.

By early 1881, however, Bright's Disease had crippled his kidneys, and on February 24, after a short illness, Henry David Cooke died at 3007 Q Street. Grace Church, which he had built in 1866, draped its facade in black for thirty days thereafter. The funeral was held at St. John's, and afterwards a memorial service at the Oak Hill Chapel preceded his burial beside Lizzie and Guy.[19]

During his remarkable career in Georgetown he was a trend-setter and a watershed figure in the town's future destiny. But not for several decades would his contribution and his influence be fully discerned and appreciated.

VI

Takeover at Oak Hill
Part One

In 1849, when William Wilson Corcoran presented Georgetown with the tract that became Oak Hill Cemetery, he never expected or wanted to become involved with its administration. He secured a good workable charter from Congress, and he did not include himself (or a personal representative such as his secretary, Anthony Hyde) among the four-man Board of Managers. His only interventions were to order improvements and make deposits into the Oak Hill account at Corcoran & Riggs. By 1853 he had lavished $56,645.69 on his dream.[1] After the completion of major construction, such as the chapel, receiving vault, massive terraces, storm sewers, roads, a retaining wall along Rock Creek, and the monumental gates and fence along R Street, he withdrew and never looked over anyone's shoulder. A similar tact characterized his many other benefactions. Indeed, he was loved and admired for it throughout the South and Washington.

But in the case of Oak Hill this attitude boomeranged. It was not until 1868, when almost twenty years had passed, that Mr. Corcoran found how neglected and irresponsible Oak Hill's bookkeeping and management had become. By then he had developed a deep commitment to the cemetery, and this kind of conduct his fastidious banker's nature could not stomach. Even worse, he found himself confronted by prejudice and personal animosity on the part of members of the Board who wanted to deflate and diminish him. During the Civil War Corcoran had been a Confederate sympathizer and still was a Democrat. Although Washington and Georgetown now coexisted in harmony despite divergent politics, the clash of wills which characterized the Oak Hill controversy caused overt hostility between the two. Politics aside, moreover, there was in fact a contest between a do-gooder and what Shakespeare called a "rascally yeaforsooth knave," such as was spawned by the Grant era administration. How the redoubtable Mr. Corcoran intervened and resolved a touchy situation constitutes the meat of this chronicle.

The problem grew out of a condition Corcoran attached to his original gift, whereby he withheld fifteen lots for his own use and for members of his and his wife's family. In 1840 his wife, Louise Morris Corcoran, died and before that, two of their three children. In 1855 he had them interred in his lot, thus driving his personal stake deeper.[2] As for himself, he was proud of being a self-made, successful banker, of having enjoyed

Takeover at Oak Hill—Part One

William Wilson Corcoran, 1798-1888 (Courtesy, Peabody Collection, Georgetown Public Library)

close friendships with seven American presidents, and of becoming famous on both sides of the Atlantic as one of the first collectors of American as well as European art. So on the tongue of land overlooking Rock Creek which included lots 1 through 15, he wanted to erect a monument to his family and also to himself. In so doing, he would also honor the city of Georgetown where he had been born in 1798 and which had given him his start.[3]

In the late 1850s his desire was only natural. It was the Romantic Age, and the presence of a well-landscaped and beautiful resting place for the dead, embellished by handsome marble and granite monuments and sculptures, enhanced a city's prestige. In an age where scarcely any museums existed and landscape architecture was in its infancy, it was also a place where people could come to improve their taste, look at art, and learn about horticulture. The first garden cemetery, Mount Auburn, dedicated in 1831 just west of Cambridge, Massachusetts, had inspired a rash of similar urban triumphs, such as Greenwood in Brooklyn, Laurel Hill in Philadelphia, and Green Mount in Baltimore.

Corcoran could not have chosen a more advantageous site than the tract he purchased from George Corbin Washington, great nephew of President George Washington. Measuring twelve and one-half acres, it cost $3,000, and was historic property. Mrs. Washington was Eliza, great-granddaughter of Col. Ninian Beall to whom the Rock of Dumbarton was patented in 1703. Her inheritance included the family seat of her father, Thomas Beall of George, identified today as 2920 R Street, and also the land just across R Street from it which became the cemetery. Road Street, as it was called then, was a rough, unimproved dirt road allowing access to several private estates on The Heights and providing a favorite afternoon and evening promenade for riders and strollers.

When he resolved to do something, Corcoran never dragged his well-shod feet. On March 3, 1849 he obtained the cemetery charter. On April 7 he met with the first Board of Managers to present the deed of conveyance and $2,000 seed-money to initiate construction. By May 8 the grounds were enclosed with a board fence to keep out wandering quadrupeds, people bent on jollification, and the curious. By May 15 George de la Roche, who had been engaged as architect and construction engineer, had already made the overall survey, assembled his crew, carts, horses, and material, and begun the work.⁴ James Renwick, Jr. was to design the Gothic Chapel. The gatehouse for the superintendent was begun, probably fashioned after a pattern from the books on Italianate domestic architecture by Andrew Jackson Downing who at the time was engaged by the federal government to draw up plans for the Washington parks. With construction progressing smoothly, the target date for the auction of lots was set for October 17, 1851. By then the gatehouse was finished, and a superintendent, John A. Blundon, an Ohio native of thirty-five years, had moved in with his family.⁵

Unhappily, no records survive of the auction at 11 a.m. on October 17. We can, however, imagine the bright autumn setting in a place famous for its oaks, people wandering about to inspect the lots, children hopping about the terraces—altogether a lively social scene with no gravestones around as yet. Like those at Mount Auburn, the paths had been named after "trees, shrubs and flowers." So it was literally possible "for those citizens later in lots 168 through 178 to go to heaven or elsewhere on the Primrose Path."⁶

We can also imagine an harassed treasurer, Lorenzo Thomas, a partner in a local flour mill, trying to mollify customers who wanted to give cash plus a note to buy a lot. According to the charter, only hard cash was acceptable. This must have proven too harsh a condition, for within a week the lots were being sold upon terms of one-third cash, with the other two-thirds to be paid in equal installments at six and nine months with interest.⁷

The change may have attracted buyers, but it complicated the bookkeeping. The bylaws called for a secretary *and* a treasurer, the latter to be at the cemetery daily to attend to the rolls and the books. The first Board of Managers ignored this stipulation, and Thomas held both jobs. Since he was paid nothing, it is not surprising that immediately after the auction he resigned.

A series of premonitory shifts followed. Walter S. Cox, an able, young lawyer, replaced Thomas, and this time, the Board voted a salary of $150 a year to the secretary-treasurer.⁸ Three years later, Cox resigned, and an experienced accountant and insurance executive took the post at a salary of $600 a year.⁹ This was Henry King, secretary of the Potomac Insurance Company at 1219 Wisconsin Avenue.¹⁰ Until then, all cemetery company records had been kept, and all meetings held, at the home of its president, John Marbury, who was also president of the Potomac Insurance Company. Since he lived at the west end of M Street, it was decided to accommodate everybody, and move the cemetery office to that of the insurance company.

John Marbury was considered a good lawyer and an effective head of the Potomac, so he presumably was aware of a rapidly increasing disorder in cemetery bookkeeping. The reason for this disarray may have lain in the insurance company's attitude that cemetery business was of secondary importance. At any rate, nine years later, in 1865, Henry King

Takeover at Oak Hill—Part One

resigned, due, he said, to failing health, and James W. Deeble took his place. Deeble, formerly a clerk at the Farmers & Mechanics Bank, replaced King in both his job as secretary of the Potomac, and as secretary of the cemetery. So naturally, the cemetery took second place again.

Meanwhile, it grew in beauty. The superintendent had started a nursery near the gatehouse for customers to select shrubs and flowers for their gravesites. He kept workmen busy all the time. Increasingly, the managers, who found the trek up Wisconsin Avenue and east on Road Street, through dust or mud, an onerous one, left administrative decisions to Blundon who appeared industrious and trustworthy, and worth his annual one thousand dollar salary.

Corcoran may have known of these changes. But he probably never looked at the records and ledgers. Moreover, during the antebellum decade, personal affairs absorbed him. He was still making his fortune and playing an active role as lobbyist and financier for the Democrats until the Whigs came in under Franklin Pierce in 1853.[11]

In 1845 he had purchased 1611 H Street, where the United States Chamber of Commerce stands now, the home of Daniel Webster when Webster was Secretary of State in the Tyler Cabinet. James Renwick, Jr., the most fashionable architect of the day, was involved in its renovation in 1849.[12] Two years later, Corcoran had constructed "hot and cold graperies for raising grapes and flowers, and a handsome brick wing attached with brownstone bay windows in the Gothic style." This wing contained a library and dining room which, after Corcoran's retirement in 1854, became a setting for his famous weekly gourmet dinners. He also gave to churches and charities and was active in local affairs. This combination of pleasure and privilege, matched by responsibility, was one Corcoran considered proper for a gentleman of his stature. Clearly, little time remained for Oak HIll.

One project, however, did bring him there. This was the construction of his family vault and monument. In 1851 Thomas U. Walter had come to Washington from Philadelphia to become Architect of the Capitol. Although the Corcoran Papers in the Library of Congress Manuscript Division do not contain any contract with Walter to design this family structure, outgoing letters to a New York importer and dealer in fine marbles, the Robert I. Brown Company, confirm it as contractor for the monument and Walter as architect and supervisor. Walter made the monument's specifications and elevations. Corcoran himself "put the Bill of Granite into the hands of three stone cutters, and asked that the bids be sent to you (Walter), not appearing myself at all."[14] In addition, at the end, Walter acted as negotiator between Corcoran and the contractor when the latter sued Corcoran for trespass.[15] His fee for this demanding role is not discussed. One reason for these gaps may have been that Walter and Corcoran moved in the same social circles, and could have arranged matters over a bottle of Corcoran's Madeira in the new library.

Corcoran also made a separate contract for a finial to top the roof

Georgetown Life, 1865-1900

of the temple. The sculptor was a young Philadelphian of Canadian birth, Isaac Broome, aged twenty-two, whom Walter may have recommended.[16] The finial was to be "of the best marble, four feet high from bottom of foot to top of head, and the price to be $500."[17] The "statue," as he called it, was a "cherub with finger pointing upward to the flight of the departed spirit, emblemized by the empty vase standing near."[18] The choice of this symbol to top an octagonal temple with eight marble Doric columns shows how the spirit of the Romantic Age had informed Corcoran's taste. The finial was evidently an afterthought, for he failed to tell Brown about it until ten months after Brown began his work.[19] The entire monument was to be complete by October 1, 1856.[20]

To synchronize this enterprise required the same tenacity, drive, and patience that had made Corcoran a successful banker. First the hole for the vault had to be dug and foundations laid. Nicholas Acker, the selected contractor for this phase of the work, was a local stonemason and Bavarian immigrant who had a stoneyard three blocks west of the Capitol.[21] Rainy weather in the fall of '56 delayed him; but finally, a year later, he finished the job and through Walter, requested payment.[22] Corcoran could have paid him, but other phases of the project proved so demanding he delayed it.

Many headaches accompanied the entire enterprise. Only after Walter's tracings for the underground vault and the elevations had been sent to Brown did Corcoran discover that they did not specify the location of the lettering.[23] So they had to be returned. On arrival they were found to be so damaged in transit as to be almost illegible, and time was wasted while new ones were made and shipped to Brown again.[24] Meantime Broome had to be kept going with $100 installments so he would have the cherub ready when the temple was ready.[25] Bad weather increased Corcoran's anxieties. "Every day's delay is important at this late state of the season," wrote Corcoran to Brown on September 7, 1857.[26] In addition to the temple, the Brown Company also had the job of cutting the marble for two family monuments Corcoran had ordered; thus, Brown had to be prodded so that the arrival of the marble elements by schooner coincided with finishing the elevation. Another chore was finding a proper derrick to hoist them into place at the site.[27] Brown was instructed to bring one to extend more than twenty-two feet.

Finally Corcoran began to see things fall into place. He must have rejoiced when "Mr. Architect Walter says he can get a derrick here."[28] But he no more than welcomed the schooner *Eliza* to the Port of Georgetown on September 29, 1857, and saw that it carried "an Italian marble monument weighing 100 tons,"[29] than he discovered Brown had not come with it as he promised. A hint of panic emanates from Corcoran's telegram to Brown. "Where are you?" he wired. "The privilege of unloading at the crane, we will be deprived of, if the matter is not attended to instantly."[30]

Soon the end was in view. On November 11 Broome was notified that the mausoleum was ready for the statue and that he should come immediately with the cherub.[31] Corcoran could now relax. He sent the sculptor $29 for "the amount of your travel, wages and board."[32] To Brown he sent the balance of $2,029 for the mausoleum.[33] Calling it a "splendid mosque," the *Evening Star* was so impressed that it said the cost would range between twenty-five and thirty thousand dollars.[34] The actual figure was "more than $13,000."[35]

The cluster of three family monuments near the temple completed what now constituted Oak Hill's most ornamental site. A massive Roman pillar was dedicated to his father Thomas, the immigrant from Limerick, Ireland, and to his mother; a plain octagonal shaft memorialized his brother Thomas, Jr., and wife Emily; and on a separate but adjacent lot, a simple upright slab with decorative cornice commemorated Commander Charles Morris, his father-in-law.

To survey this scene, this commitment to his past and to what he regarded as the heart and essence of his gift, one can imagine him picking his cautious way over uneven terrain to the opposite slope, a commanding figure in black, with gold-tipped stick and stovepipe hat. Through the bare branches of the oaks, he saw many monuments reminiscent of long and valued friendships: in a formal circle, the column of blueish variegated European marble, made in Sweden, topped with the winged angel, dedicated to the Baron Alexandre de Bodisco who died in 1854; to the northwest, beside the Corcoran lots, a miniature Gothic canopy enclosing the figure of a girl, a dove at her feet, the child of Corcoran's friend and business associate, William M. Gwin, Senator from California in 1852; in the crook of a nearby slope, the lot where Jefferson Davis had buried his boy, marked only by spirea in bloom and lilies of the valley. Here stood a pillar with cloth draped over the edge, there a mourning maiden with head bowed over an urn, and beyond, a mossy lectern with tasseled pillow, stone prayerbook open to the weather. Altogether it was a sight to comfort and gladden his Romantic heart.

VII

Takeover at Oak Hill
Part Two

The widower W. W. Corcoran may have been comforted and gladdened by the sight of his family monuments on Lots 1 through 15 at Oak Hill, but its peace and that of Corcoran himself were soon to be shattered. When the Civil War broke out, Georgetown was overrun with the military. Soldiers raced their horses along Road Street, cracked whips over mules and wagons, and took potshots at the stained glass windows of the Chapel. Between 1857 and 1861 the Board of Managers did not meet, avoiding the trek up to the cemetery and leaving matters to Blundon. Finally on June 19, 1862, and perhaps at Corcoran's suggestion, the lotholders broke a lapse of five years to hold an annual meeting.[1] Corcoran was elected one of the four managers, and he accepted the nomination. To understand this singular move, we must backtrack.

During the first year of the Civil War, the whole warp and woof of his life was torn apart. Although epitomizing the old southern gentleman and Democrat, Corcoran had never supported slavery, always putting the defense of the Union first. But since Corcoran & Riggs had been the only large bank between New Orleans and Philadelphia, his business interests had led him into fast friendships with leading southern bankers.

In addition, in 1859, his only daughter, Louise, married George Eustis, Jr., Congressman from Louisiana, who, after the war began, became private secretary to John Slidell, the Confederate Envoy to France. Many close friends left Washington or were inaccessible in the Confederacy. Corcoran himself became so suspect that he could not object when the federal government requisitioned Harewood, his country estate, for a hospital, and his art gallery, now known as the Renwick Gallery, begun in 1859 at Seventeenth and Pennsylvania Avenues and by 1861 only roofed in, for a clothing depot. All these factors determined him to ship his fortune abroad and follow himself. By renting it to the French Consul, he saved his house.[2]

After his election to the Oak Hill board on June 19, 1862, Corcoran told the three other members he expected to be absent for some time and requested the appointment of a confidential friend and agent (Anthony Hyde, his secretary since 1847) as a temporary replacement.[3] The president, John Marbury, was an outright southern sympathizer whose support he might have expected. But the other two were Union men. So, uncertain about succeeding in his request, he sent his secretary out to obtain

Takeover at Oak Hill—Part Two

twelve proxies as support.[4] Evidently aware of what he was up to, the others produced thirty-five proxies and defeated him, but did allow him the small comfort of seeing his name remain on the Board.[5] He passed the summer in Washington, arranging to convert his fortune into cash and then into pounds sterling and to ship it via the Cunard Line to George Peabody in London, a friend and banker living there who had started his career in Georgetown at the same time as Corcoran. By October 8 he had sailed to be gone for the duration.[6]

During his exile, the cemetery expanded to its maximum. Blundon had worked hard to lay out the other hillsides, and all lots were sold by March 13, 1863.[7] Seven thousand five hundred interments had been made.[8] Even portions of the hitherto inviolate lawns and avenues were laid out for sale.[9] With space so valuable, it is not surprising that negotiations began to purchase six acres of land adjoining the cemetery on the east from the Evermay estate, owned by Charles and Elizabeth Dodge. Dodge asked $8,000 for the parcel and got it.[10] Corcoran did not learn of this until his return in 1865.

At that time, in September, many complex readjustments confronted him. Foremost lay the disagreeable prospect of retrieving his fortune and his real estate. As the most prominent Confederate sympathizer who had left his country and taken his money with him, he had returned under a cloud. As a Democrat he now had to ingratiate himself into an unfamiliar Washington society dominated by Republicans. His loyalty was still in doubt.

A visit to the cemetery, hitherto a comfort, now became an ordeal. During his absence many unfamiliar monuments near his own had been erected to Union officers, and the place wore an alien cast.[11] In the next two years he attended most meetings of the cemetery board, but in spite of hearing decisions made of which he did not approve, he remained unassertive. One in which he did take part involved a second purchase of Evermay land, comprising seven acres, he was told, and costing $10,000. Corcoran recommended a preliminary survey, and then paying, instead of the lump sum, $1,000 an acre. On September 3, 1867, this motion was passed unanimously.[12] Soon thereafter, having received word that his daughter's health was worsening, Corcoran sailed for Cannes, France. Only six months later, when he returned with her remains, did he discover that his motion had been ignored, and the land bought anyway without a survey and at the price Dodge had asked.[13]

One reason for Corcoran's restraint was the disconcerting presence of a new board member elected in 1867 whose close ties with the current Republican regime made him a potential threat to Corcoran's efforts to regain his real estate. Captain William P. S. Sanger was a full-blooded Yankee born in Massachusetts in 1810,[14] whose career as a civil engineer began in 1834 in Boston where he built a stone drydock so well he was transferred to Norfolk, Virginia, to build another one. In 1843 he was posted to the Washington Navy Yard and its Bureau of Yards and Docks.

Georgetown Life, 1865-1900

George de la Roche, Oak Hill's architect, had been a draughtsman there, along with other Georgetowners. Consequently, by 1867, when Sanger became Chief Engineer, his acquaintances attracted him to Georgetown where in that year he moved his family to 3309 Prospect Avenue.[15]

After his election to the cemetery board, Sanger lost no time in turning another manager into his rubberstamp. George W. Beall, a merchant tailor, probably respected his competence excessively. Callahan's *List of Officers of the U.S. Navy and the U.S. Marine Corps, 1775-1900* does not mention a Captain Sanger.[16] So Sanger's title must have been complimentary. But his continuing use of it suggests an arrogance which would have set Corcoran's Irish hackles up. Corcoran could not afford, however, to jeopardize Sanger's goodwill, and supported him in engaging surveyors to plat the grounds so that lotholders with 300 square feet or more would know they were qualified to vote at the annual meeting. Corcoran also supported placing the company's books under the control of an accountant.

After his daghter was buried at Oak Hill on February 17, 1868, Corcoran looked through the scrapbooks Hyde had kept for him during his absence. They contained news clippings of events Corcoran had missed. In this way he learned about the purchase of the second Dodge parcel and what Dodge was paid for it. He also read how majestic oaks and tulip poplars had been felled, monuments toppled off their bases, and "how the hillside looked like the laying off of a city of building lots. Why not leave nature unharmed?" asked the *Daily Intelligencer*.[17]

All his life a man of action, Corcoran moved independently, without telling the Board, to hire his own surveyor, Henry Brewer of Georgetown, to measure the two Dodge tracts. Brewer found the first bought in 1865 to measure 3 1/4 acres, instead of the six the company had paid for, and the second purchased in 1867, 4.09 acres instead of the seven entered in the books.[18]

Aware now of shifty treatment and of what could happen behind his back, Corcoran requested again at the lotholders' meeting in June the appointment of a named friend to represent him at meetings, so he could be spared the long trek over and back. Expecting this request, the thirty-five lotholders who did attend had been handpicked, and came armed with enough proxies to defeat him. Two weeks later, unexpected support cropped up. The *Georgetown Courier* was a conservative Democratic newspaper with a wide local readership. On June 27, its editorial "acknowledged that the ordeal from which our country is just emerging had tended to blunt and render callous all finer feelings. We submit that such abuse of Mr. Corcoran's wishes is regretful."[19]

Nevertheless, an aggravating series of reverses followed. On July 2 Corcoran revealed to the board his plan to build a substantial wall along Mill Street around the new addition to the cemetery. A gate and lodge would be built where Mill Street met the Creek. Since he had financed all other enclosures, he wanted to do so again. But first, the lines should be surveyed and specifications drawn up.[20] Marbury, Sanger and Beall, however, made no motion to this effect, nor did they express appreciation. Corcoran then departed for his annual summer holiday at White Sulphur Springs with Robert E. Lee. On his return, he found that the Board had ignored his offer and continued on the course, initiated even as he made his proposal, of building the wall according to their own plans.[21]

Ensuing slaps and snubs compounded his frustration. Starkweather & Plowman, the engineers whom Sanger had engaged to plat the cemetery, delivered their map. The lots showed no measurements. Corcoran asked why not, and they said: "Because Sanger said they were not needed."[22] Corcoran tried to obtain from Blundon an accounting on all lots laid out, an inventory of tools and implements owned by the cemetery, and a listing of the employees. Blundon answered he had kept none.[23] William H. King, the accountant hired to examine the books, said he could not continue without assistance, they were in such a state of disorder. Corcoran immediately offered to appoint a separate treasurer, bond him and pay his costs. The other members voted "No," Sanger moving that the board authorize no more expenditures for services of this kind.[24]

On November 14, John Marbury resigned as president. He was extremely deaf and in poor health, and had tried to resign for several years. But since it was convenient to keep him there and thus prevent Corcoran from moving in, the Board members, except for Corcoran, had refused to accept his resignation. Now, however, his health was so bad that they had no alternative but to do so. And in a startling about-face they elected Corcoran in his place.

But if Corcoran thought that now at last he had the right to inspect the books, he was mistaken. Sanger and his friends probably hoped to handle him as they had his predecessor, and so the secretary, J. W. Deeble, told Corcoran that he could *not* examine the books. The books were HIS.[25] Only a decision of the whole board could release them. Sanger and Beall also nominated Alexander R. Shepherd, Sanger's kinsman, to replace Marbury as a manager.[26] This was highly irregular, and Corcoran said so, because by charter only lotholders could elect a manager. But Shepherd was told his vote could count, and he came to meetings anyway.

This addition emphasized the political aura now investing cemetery matters. In 1868 the forcible Shepherd was such a close friend of President Grant that he belonged in the latter's "Kitchen Cabinet." For eight years Corcoran's requests for back rent for his art gallery had been rejected, and he had had to tread delicately when confronting powerful Republicans, but he was made of resilient stuff. Outraged by these obstructions in an area where he had shown himself eminently knowledgeable, that of accounting and record-keeping, he now approached the public press, and took his gloves off.

In a long editorial after the New Year the *Georgetown Courier* described the banker's efforts to have the books examined and said "the board was determined to prevent this, and that committees were appointed only to have their powers removed."[27] Sanger and Beall countered with a pam-

Georgetown Life, 1865-1900

phlet charging that Corcoran's sole object was to dismiss the superintendent.[28] Corcoran declared in the *Courier* he was not guilty of such paltry malice. "That I am obliged thus to defend myself publicly before the people of Georgetown is under the circumstances extremely painful to me." He then requested the lotholders to meet and say whether their rights should be respected or not.[29]

Up to this point the Washington press had confined its coverage of this conflict to short news items. But now the *Intelligencer* compared Corcoran to King Lear and pointed out the "wisdom on the part of future public benefactors of retaining the power to prevent defeat of their generous purposes."[30]

A bizarre incident at the cemetery gave the *Star* a chance to outdo its rival. During January Corcoran had been able to read the Letterbooks and found harsh language to people with relatives stored in the vault, saying that unless dues were paid, the bodies would be buried in some remote corner difficult to find. Corcoran asked the superintendent where the relatives were buried. Blundon pointed to a grave by the roadside. "They are right there," he said, "both in one grave."

> "I immediately directed their removal," declared Corcoran, "to my own lot at my expense. After a week this hadn't been done. The superintendent explained that without an order from the secretary and a resolution passed, they could not be removed until vault dues were paid, the lady's being $178.50 and the child's $940. A friend offered to pay in compromise $100 for the child which was accepted. I offered the same which was also accepted and paid by me. Not even the removal was permitted until burial fees were paid in advance by order of the board."[31]

The *Star* then quoted *Genesis*, Chapter 23, verses 9-23, describing Abraham's purchase of the field of Machpelah which had a cave where he buried his wife Sarah.[32] The entire episode so agitated Corcoran that he declined to meet again with the board until the lotholders' meeting.[33]

This meeting was scheduled for Monday, February 15, 1869, at 5 p.m. Remembering his defeat by proxies in June 1862, Corcoran had his secretary scour Georgetown six days before, to round up well over one hundred proxies in support of creating an impartial Investigating Committee to examine the books and make a report.[34] The supportive *Intelligencer* ran a long editorial that morning "to arrest the attention of the lotholders to the very imperfect manner in which the records, the financial affairs, and the cemetery grounds have been for a long series of years managed."[35]

Corcoran needn't have worried. "The meeting," commented the *Courier*, "was the most imposing in point of numbers in respect of solid worth, that ever was convened in this city."[36] An investigating committee was appointed and given full powers of examination, and Corcoran was asked to submit his charges in writing. Randolph Coyle, still another surveyor, was appointed to measure the lots and list those qualified to vote in June, all to be ready by late May.

In one way these trying events served as distractions for Corcoran who was preparing for the return of his capital from Europe. The bulk of it arrived between May 3 and June 9, a period when almost $700,000 was brought back.[37] To surmount the government's lingering animosity, he had decided to donate his private art collection and the gallery itself to the public. He designated a Board of Trustees who applied to Congress for a charter of incorporation, and then established a trust with this huge sum to maintain the gifts. The trust freed the gallery from taxation and resulted in partial recovery of back rent.[38]

Consequently on May 25, he must have rejoiced to see the crowd packing the markethouse hall to hear the investigating committee's report on his charges. The major ones were:

> The Board had not had the superintendent's books examined since 1849.
>
> The Board had allowed arrearages of almost $12,000 to accumulate, uncollected.
>
> The Board had purchased six acres in 1865 at the highly inflated price of $8,000, and then gone to great pains to have 3 1/4 acres omitted from the deed of conveyance. As a result, many lots were sold and persons buried in land to which the cemetery had no title.
>
> The Board allowed the superintendent to receive and enter all fees in the books in gross.
>
> The Board had collaborated with a Philadelphia stone-cutting firm to establish a monument salesyard across Road Street on Col. Carter's lot (the SW corner of 30th and R Streets), and then had the superintendent be its agent, thus cutting out local competition.

The committee sustained eighteen of the twenty-two charges. It could not agree, however, that any intentional injustices had been done by the superintendent, and concluded that "As 'to err is human, and to amend is divine,' harmony may yet be restored."[39]

A week later, June 7, the surveyor's plat and the list of qualified voters were ready, and local excitement had risen to fever-pitch. Still obsessed with lining up votes, Corcoran revealed he knew how to operate too. Monday afternoon he transferred lots two through fifteen of his entire cemetery property to fourteen friends, keeping lot number 1, where the Doric temple was, for his own, thus securing fifteen votes for fifteen lots where formerly he would have had only one vote for the entire area. (Then soon after the meeting and the crucial vote, the fourteen lots were deeded back to him for one dollar each.[40]) In addition, he sent Hyde out again on a

Georgetown Life, 1865-1900

Sunday safari, the day before the meeting, to bring in one hundred and twenty-five more votes or proxies.

First on the agenda was reading the list of qualified voters. The letter "G" was nearly concluded when Mr. Corcoran stood up and announced his name had not been called. The secretary, James W. Deeble, explained that because of the fourteen transfers of lots the honorable gentleman had made that day, he had deprived himself of the right to vote. Reference to the plat showed that Mr. Corcoran still owned four hundred square feet and could vote. He rose to do so. Immediately, George Hill, a local papermill owner, popped up to dispute his right, "I claim the right," said Mr. Corcoran, "even if the objection comes from a man who possesses two lots, upon neither of which he has paid a dollar."

Amid much excitement, the choleric Mr. Hill leapt from his seat on the extreme east of the room, advanced rapidly toward Mr. Corcoran who sat on a front bench west, and shook his hand in his face. Mr. Corcoran remained seated and perfectly collected. "With all respect to you, Sir," cried Hill, "I pronounce your statement false. It is false, Sir!" James M. Corcoran, the banker's nephew, rushed up, brandishing his cane, but the interposition of friends prevented a collision. Hill then crossed the hall, intending to vote, and looking defiance. As he approached, almost all those on the west seats rose, and Fred W. Jones clasped him in his arms to prevent another collision. Order restored, Judge Advocate R. T. Merrick said the dignity of the meeting had been compromised, but he would continue the balloting and at its close inquire if Mr. Hill had paid up. Applause met these remarks. Mr. Hill departed without voting. The ballot gave Mr. Corcoran the victory, and the *Courier*'s editor wrapped up the event with the punchline: "Mr. Corcoran's opponents sustained a Waterloo defeat!"[41]

The new members of the Board of Managers replaced Corcoran's three opponents, and the next afternoon he called them to the gatehouse to elect a new superintendent, Daniel Barker, formerly assistant superintendent of the Experimental Garden at the Department of Agriculture in Washington.[42]

Corcoran remained as president until 1872. Then, stating that the place would be well run by the next president, Charles M. Matthews, an able, responsible, loyal Georgetown lawyer, and the books kept to his satisfaction, he resigned. His takeover had been a success.

VIII

"The Impregnable Burg"

Anyone who had to travel through Metro construction sites in the District of Columbia during the mid-70s will appreciate what Georgetowners contended with between 1871 and 1873 when the Board of Public Works was reconstructing the town's hilly face. Fortunately, for today's historian, the *Georgetown Courier*'s editor, John D. McGill, was an energetic and literate fellow with a true reporter's curiosity, relish for detail, and nose for a good story. He inspected the chaotic scene day and night, planted correspondents in the embattled sectors, and churned out the news with humor and compassion. In winter he worked like a troglodyte in a subterranean cave five feet below street level without water or heat.[1] At one time, when the marketplace on M Street was being graded, he was submerged below fifteen feet of dirt, gravel and clay. Despite these circumstances he stayed there because his location next door to two livery stables, a carriage manufactory, barber shops, and a popular restaurant-saloon, all run by gregarious sons of Erin, made 3285 M Street a nerve- and news-center. His office was where the action was.

When the BPW under Alexander "Boss" Shepherd started to cut its swathe in the summer of 1871, Riley Shinn, the Irish manufacturer of ales, porter and brown stout on Olive Street, sold his lucrative business and bought the Union Hotel. After remodeling it, he turned to street paving contracts. Among Boss Shepherd's first moves was to set Shinn and his crew to work digging up M Street west to the Union Hotel site at the intersection of 30th Street. Here the picks and shovels hit a stratum of Ninian Beall's Rock of Dumbarton, and in blasting their way through it, bashed in a sewer leaving a gaping orifice from which mephitic gasses escaped throughout the winter. Shinn tore his red hair at this catastrophe, for since the new territorial government was just getting under way, he was expecting his Pocket Tuileries to welcome honored visitors and assemblages. Now they couldn't possibly set foot in the place.

As usual, McGill found remunerative aspects in every turn of event.

> Crowds of experts, inexperts and quidnuncs stood about the holes, peeling and eating oranges. Supervisors would be wise to keep this blasting going to engage the attentions of these well-meaning loafers who know just how to drop a peel to evade the

Georgetown Life, 1865-1900

eye and catch the foot. So many foot pavements were torn up that Georgetowners came to be known by their walk, the 'gait of a horse with a spring-halt.'[2]

In July 1872 Boss Shepherd and Governor Cooke came to "inspect the fortifications, visit Mullett's Gap and Forts Cooke and Magruder."[3] (A. B. Mullet and James Magruder were important officials in the new government.) Here they found that a big hump in the M Street grade, which had been there "since the beginning of time," had been removed, and that now the view across the Creek into Washington was at last uninterrupted. They found Buckey & Marbury's Hardware Store, which stood where the Georgetown Branch of the National Bank of Washington now is, several feet above the temporary sidewalk. Walking further west, they discovered the brick markethouse, built in 1865, submerged under the rubble heaps necessary to build up M Street so that Wisconsin could flow smoothly into it. Another encounter was with the German confectioner, Fred Stohlman, whose horse had sunk in the M Street mud. When the rider was dug out, he said this was his first introduction to the BPW, and swore it would be his last.[4] From his cave fifteen feet below the street, McGill declared that "this ancient burg is becoming impregnable."[5]

Mounting the piles, McGill watched the stupendous undertaking of hoisting the new markethouse up to the altered grade. The structure measured 246' 8" long by 40' 8" wide. Two months were spent inserting jack-screws into the supporting foundations. Then in ten days mules tugged at ropes attached to a winch to elevate the structure 13' 3" to conform to the altered grade, leaving the icehouse and restaurant underneath at street-level.[6]

An epidemic horse disease, which for lack of a better name was called "hippmania, epizooti, epihippic, etc.," brought all maneuvers to a halt. It was early November 1872, and Washington was gearing up to celebrate Grant's election to a second term. "I left the White House between 1 and 2 a.m.," wrote Henry Cooke to Jay, his brother, November 6, 1872, "and we had to walk home to Georgetown, there being no horses fit for service. Business is virtually suspended. Successful politicians and other folk had to forego the luxury of carriages, stages and street cars for many days. The streets were silent except for the patter of human feet."[7] The only people glad to see the familiar piles of dirt flanking the Georgetown street were those walking at night from Washington since the piles told them they were back at home.[8]

At length, though, the disease abated, the markethouse was elevated, and with the "agricultural experiments" completed as far west as Potomac Street, the timetable called for moving axes, picks, shovels, saws, carts and horses to N Street west of Wisconsin. Here lived many of the residents paying the highest taxes. Along the north side were twenty-odd handsome brick dwellings built in the federal era, and on the south, ten or fifteen more, with a population of perhaps fifty leading families, including lawyers,

"The Impregnable Burg"

millers, physicians, federal clerks and lumber merchants. Boasting that their street was one of the "finest in town, most popular leading as it does to Georgetown College, to the Holy Trinity Church and its Convent, and to the Visitation Academy,"[9] they petitioned the BPW *not* to use the round block pavements, and to give the street a carriageway. Their petition was granted, but at a cost, it turned out, of temporary total immobility. Mary S. Sweeny, born in Connecticut in 1810, wanted friends east of Wisconsin Avenue to know what life in the beleaguered community was like. So, signing her articles MSS, she began reportage in the *Georgetown Courier* on August 31, 1872, when the work force encountered its first formidable obstacle.

This obstacle, a towering sycamore planted in 1820, had a root structure that spread east and west under the dirt road in front of Smith Row where the Sweenys lived at 3265. Old Syc, standing one hundred feet high, was a beacon at night with its light mottled bark and an aviary by day for local birds as well as those in migration. The local children loved it so much that sometimes three or four little boys would join hands and, stretching their arms around its ten-foot girth, give the old fellow a hug.

To reach the roots the workmen dug an immense pit nineteen feet deep which became a tremendous topic of conversation. While peering down into its depths, reminiscent of the "last home of all," ladies forgot the latest fashions, weather, and servants, and even the annoyance of "musquitoes". Depressed by the sight and unable to get away from the sawing and hacking sounds from down below, the neighborhood found it refreshing to see even a wandering cow or a fat young porker perambulating about.

By September 28, Old Syc lay prostrate and headless, its body reaching diagonally across the street, its head on marble steps. Where the wood was cut, it presented a peculiar grainy look, like a piece of beefsteak. Just before it fell, poor Polly Green, a neighbor's parrot, "snapped asunder" [sic] on her perch. Shock at the sound of blows against the tree had killed her. Caught up in this neighborhood tragedy, friends called to talk about Polly and reminisce about how, when they came for breakfast, she would hop onto the table and nibble luscious grapes on their plates. After this episode, time dragged until finally, on December 7, MSS got her wish. N Street was now paved and had a carriageway down the middle. $50,043.90 had been spent to make N Street West the finest residential street in Georgetown.[10]

Simultaneously, the hilly topography east of Wisconsin Avenue was suffering equally drastic changes. Work began on N Street East between 31st and 30th Streets in June 1873, and by July the north line had been cut down five feet. This is why the handsome twin brick dwellings at 3025 and 3027, built that spring by Dr. John S. Billings and his brother-in-law Oscar Stevens, were left elevated above the sidewalk, allowing for one of the most graceful entrances in Georgetown, a wrought-iron horseshoe-curving stairway up to the front doors. Across the street at sidewalk level was the austere federal architecture of 3038 N Street, a striking contrast, and typical of Georgetown's incorrigible yet always attractive diversity.

By spring Dumbarton Avenue, one block north, had also been cut down ten to twelve feet and given neatly laid sidewalks and a carriageway.[11] Objections were raised about the amount of money expended on this sparsely traveled street. But at the time Mrs. Ellen Boggs and her son William Brenton Boggs, Paymaster of the U.S. Navy, owned 3035 Dumbarton Avenue with its large house and almost parklike surrounding grounds (which would lie undeveloped until after 1900). She was a large taxpayer and one to be cossetted.

Three blocks further east, Herring Hill found itself almost buried. Streets leading into the region, where houses had been built following the lay of the land, were leveled. So much dirt and gravel were hauled from all other excavations and dumped onto Monroe (or 27th) Street, that Square 46 at the south corner bordering Rock Creek became a dump, and then, in the 80s, the official Public Dump. In the late fall of 1872 the District Assessor found houses along 27th "inaccessible and thirty feet or more of dirt piled to the roof-levels."[12] One owner endured the siege. Others moved to West Georgetown near the College walls, where in turn they were pushed out by the dumping of more rubble when the west terminals of N, O, and P Streets were graded. The damage to east Georgetown was so patent that even J. D. McGill sympathized. "And they still have to pay taxes on their properties. It just isn't fair, especially since they are not even favored with a sewer."[13]

In West Georgetown, at the same time, a different outfit for a different reason was piling up "Egyptian pyramids and Indian mounds" along O and P Streets from Wisconsin to 35th Street. The Metropolitan Rail Road Company, which had merged with the Connecticut Avenue and Park Railway Company and the Union Railway Company, in 1872 was laying its combined right-of-way from Connecticut to Georgetown and return. As soon as the P Street bridge was completed in the fall of 1871, the company laid out its Georgetown route along P to Wisconsin, then jogged diagonally across to Volta Place and continued on to 35th. But it acted too hastily. The area at the corner of 33rd and Volta Place was very congested, with over 100 Negroes living in the row of Twenty Buildings, many of them descendants of the free Negroes who had settled there before 1840. Moreover, back of the Twenty Buildings, where Volta Place Playground lies now, stretched the bleak, festering and offensively smelling thickets of the old Presbyterian Cemetery, first dedicated in 1802, with its fallen gravestones and vandalized graves. Its burial vault a short distance back from the corner (its location has never been determined) was neither tight nor empty. The situation was so disagreeable that when in 1873 William W. Corcoran, thinking to do his hometown a favor, had the remains of Dr. Stephen Bloomer Balch, beloved pastor of the Bridge Street Presbyterian Church, transferred and buried at the 33rd Street cemetery, he had them disinterred a year later and removed to Oak Hill, a much more agreeable place for this revered figure to repose.[14]

"The Impregnable Burg"

So in 1872 a more fortunate route was worked out for the streetcars. The rails so hastily laid down in the mud were dug out and placed in less populous P Street with its wide views of substantial brick houses and, especially, of the Hezekiah Magruder garden at 3315 P where, against a background of pines, hemlock, and spruce, the Magruders had roses, larkspur, camellias, and stock, growing in borders and clumps.[15] The high banks on the north side, where sit today the row houses built in the 1890s, indicate how the street had to be cut down to accommodate the railroad. Today the Georgetown University bus follows this precise route over to the University and back.

After all this digging and filling, how did Georgetown look in 1873? "The Bewildered Dutchman" whom McGill encountered can tell you.

> Vat ish de matter mit de houses, said a Dutchman who had come to town since the improvements started. Houses have got de St. Vitus dance, for some, dey chump up and dey chump down. One little house he chump up on de high hill, and a big house he leap down in de valley. Some houses dey be two stories, now dey stretch up tree, and even four. Dey stand on stilts and de beoples make piles under dem like it was one Amsterdam![16]

The cost of these "improvements" may seem excessive. By March 1875, $8,041,542.96 had been spent all over the city of Washington, including Georgetown. The latter's total was $1,139,767. In addition, $8,687 had been spent for planting trees and placing around each one a protective whitewashed box.[17] But it was these changes that established the very diverse topography which today, in the small, compact community of 595.8 acres, offers a graceful and challenging setting for almost every architecural twist and adjustment produced in the innovative 19th century.

IX

"Georgetown at a Standpoint"

Indeed by 1875, Georgetown's appearance had altered so radically that people said if Rip Van Winkle were to wake up, he would find it changed from a country village into a city.[1] This could almost have been true, if Rip didn't wander out to peripheral Georgetown.

The poorer districts had been completely ignored. In the western sector near Holy Trinity Church and the College, a thousand Irish lived in poverty so patent that the enumerator for the 1870 census bracketed seven households on the south side of O Street between 35th and 36th Streets and wrote in the comment: "These people are very poor," a rare thing for him to do.[2] Here the space between the rows of houses remained dirt and rubble without benefit of gutter, sewer, or streetlight. The same situation prevailed in the eastern part of Georgetown where blacks lived in a web of dirt lanes, the squalor occasionally relieved by a modest, two-story dwelling erected by a Virginia carpenter or a thrifty Negro of local background.

Had the poor considered it, they could have relished the fact that the northern extremity where lived some of the richest people, like the Linthicum and the Peck families, remained equally neglected. While access to the High Service Reservoir at the corner of Wisconsin Avenue and R Street (where the Public Library stands now) and to the adjacent Scott property was graveled, the remainder of R (or Road) Street, was left a wide dirt lane full of holes and ruts until around 1900.[3] However, the steep grade up Wisconsin from the waterfront had been immensely improved and was cobbled, bricked, and guttered. Horses hauled their loads up with ease and, by the same token, runaways found this descent an irresistible invitation, even though a plunge or a smash into the Passeno boathouse or the Pickrells' warehouses at the bottom awaited them. Moreover, new sidewalks lined the avenue and pedestrians soon discovered what they were for.

Beyond Road Street where the Tenallytown Road began, the countryside opened out into the undulating pastures and meadows belonging to the powerful clan of Georgetown butchers such as the Weavers and the Kenglas. The role the butchers played in the preservation of Georgetown cannot be underestimated. Because of their longtime monopoly of the real estate between R and Calvert Street, developers could not invade the land-

"Georgetown at a Standpoint"

scape west of Massachusetts Avenue, nor could Georgetown expand to the north. Its only opening was to the northwest through the Richard S. Cox estate of sixty-five acres on Hickory Nut Hill which eventually became Burleith.[4]

Thus the town had to grow within itself. Small neighborhoods and communities developed around a corner store, a shop, or a church, where people met regularly and could sustain friendships. Before the BPW phase and the introduction in 1874 of the Metropolitan Rail Road's crosstown horse-car route, it was difficult to get about. Residents in northeast Georgetown, for instance, felt isolated and trapped. Now sidewalks, better walking conditions on drained streets, and the chance to move from one side of town to the other with ease extended the scope of their lives.

The streetscape was immeasurably improved. Looking east toward Rock Creek from the marketplace, one could now see over the trees along Rock Creek straight through to Washington. The venerable F & M Bank at the corner of 31st and M streets had put on a new coat of paint and replaced its faded old sign with a new and clearly lettered one.[5] South of M, 29th Street, which had always been a precarious and muddy stretch, was paved and bricked so that coal and ice carts traveled without mishap. K Street was paved its entire length. With its riverwall complete and many new wharves built, it had once more become a busy thoroughfare, with schooners and steamers arriving daily with wooden paving blocks for Washington, tar melters, and yellow and white pine from Maine for the Libbeys' lumberyards.[6] Indeed, during the Centennial Year many citizens took their families to Philadelphia and found themselves boasting about being part of the best-paved city in the nation.

The erection and opening of Curtis School on O Street opposite St. John's Episcopal Church also boosted local pride. A string of rickety frame and brick tenements housing refugee blacks was torn down, and the school was built with $50,000 appropriated by the Territorial government. Inside, on the first floor, was the Peabody Library. For ten years the *Courier* had lamented the lack of a place where the idle could go, intellectuals could find stimulus, and evening meetings could be held. George Peabody made his gift of $15,000 seed money for a circulating library in 1867. But despite the power and prestige of the principal trustees, William W. Corcoran and George W. Riggs, nothing had been done about it.[7] Now everyone could rejoice in a library of one thousand books, with more coming in daily, selected by Ainsworth Spofford, Librarian of Congress.[8] As the first institution in Georgetown designated for community use, for rich or poor, black or white, young or old, it held a special significance.

On the most important residential streets a building boom was gathering momentum. Several factors accounted for this. A few large property owners, like Esau Pickrell and Mrs. Eliza Mosher, died, and the next generation subdivided the property and built dwellings for sale or rent. Esau Pickrell's widow Virginia, for example, lost no time in working with her son-in-law, Boyd Smith, to build a brace of five handsome French-attic row dwellings on 33rd Street, Nos. 1418-1426, which were sold or rented almost immediately. Newcomers constituted an ever-growing market, and demand for housing exceeded supply.

The Bodisco property at 3322 O Street, composed of two large lots—the house on Lot 113 and the vacant contiguous Lot 114—offered another variation. In 1838 the Baron Alexandre de Bodisco came to Washington as Envoy Extraordinary and Minister Plenipotentiary from Russia. Born in 1786, he was still a bachelor. Needing a suitable mansion for entertaining, he bought 3322 O Street. At a Christmas party given for his nephews, Waldemar and Boris, he met the beautiful Harriet Beall Williams, third daughter of a long established local family and a belle of sixteen tender years. Falling

3127 Dumbarton Avenue was built by Charles H. Cragin, Jr., attorney and great-grandson of Henry Foxall

madly in love with her, he eventually proposed. Although opposing the match, her parents at length gave in, and "Beauty and the Beast," as the gossips called the pair, were married in her home on R Street on April 9, 1840. The marriage was happy and productive. Four sons, some of whom were educated in Russia, two daughters, and the still lovely young widow mourned the Baron when he died early in 1854 and was buried at Oak Hill Cemetery. In his will he "thanked my dear wife for having embellished my life and wish with my whole heart that hers may continue without clouds until the last moment of her life." He urged her to remarry and make another man as happy as she had made him.

This Harriet did, in 1860. She married Capt. Douglas Gordon Scott, former military attaché at the British Ministry. He had since been posted to Madras, India, and it was there he took his bride.

After the Civil War they returned briefly to Georgetown. During her marriage to the Baron, Harriet had become a land-rich woman. As a wedding present he had signed 3322 over to her. Later, in 1850, at public auction and undoubtedly with his sanction and money, she had bought from the Clement Smith heirs the vacant lot, No. 114, to the east, the site of 3314 and 3318 O Street today. During his lifetime he had also bought the property to the west at 3328 O Street, with the charming little brick dwelling familiar to many Georgetowners today as Bernard Wyckoff's home.

Now back in Georgetown, Harriet sold off some of this property. In

"Georgetown at a Standpoint"

1867 Abraham Herr, a flour miller, bought 3322, and Captain William P. S. Sanger, Corcoran's current adversary, bought Lot 114, the vacant lot. After these transactions were completed, the Scotts left for England to live on the Isle of Wight. From there, in 1876, she sold the remaining property, 3328 O Street, to a Treasury clerk. Thus the colorful and remantic Bodisco story passed into the rich limbo of Georgetown legend.[9]

In disposing of his new property, Sanger acted in character as a wheeler-dealer. First he had it subdivided. Then in 1871 he sold the east half to Holmes Offley, a stockbroker and friend of Henry Cooke, who built the formal house now on the lot for $6,000. Three years later he sold the other half to a buyer who immediately sold it to Robert Hunter, a shoemaker with Civil Wartime savings to spend. Hunter put up a dwelling at 3318 also costing $6,000.[10] (In 1979 it sold for $505,000.) On the opposite side of the street, a local grocer built 3331 O, just west of the Pickrell house and its gardens.[11] At the time and until 1893, when the brownstone row on the north side was erected, the neighborhood must have been a charming and green section of town, almost suburban in character.

Across Wisconsin Avenue in the neighborhood of P and 31st Streets, the same pattern was repeated. For a long time P had been a pleasant wide street with venerable brick dwellings built neat and square on the south sidewalk, with gardens behind.[12] Looking north, east of 31st, residents could enjoy the view of the Dodge farm with its spacious house on the northern corner at Q Street built in 1812. But now the mistress of all that property, Miss Emily Dodge, was in her late sixties and needed money. Ever since her father, Francis Dodge, died in 1852, she had kept house for various and sundry brothers (and their wives), nephews, nieces, and brothers-in-law such as Ben: Perley Poore, a noted journalist, who used her as a postbox. Now the larder was growing sparse. Simultaneously, the Libbey brothers, J. Edward and Joseph, had grown prosperous and wanted large fashionable establishments. So Miss Emily sold them two contiguous parcels where a pear orchard was in its prime. In 1877 they erected their brick dwellings, side by each,

The Bodisco House at 3322 O Street when it was an apartment house with ten units in the early 1900s.

50

Georgetown Life, 1865-1900

at 3043 and 3053 P Street. (Only 3053 remains today, much altered.)[13]

The opposite corners had also been filled in. The Georgetown Improvement Company was formed to buy vacant lots, erect suitable dwellings, and offer them for sale with a small advance on the cost of construction.[14] Its first purchase was Judge Morsell's yard where Miss Lipscomb's select school for girls had practiced calisthenics or whatever young girls of that era did in recess. Now they had to move out to permit construction of a stylish row of four tall narrow brick dwellings. Henry P. Gilbert, the former secondhand hardware merchant, took the choice lot, 3100, at the corner, at which event some of the neighboring oldtimers must have tut-tutted and shaken their heads, for he was a parvenu. (Only five years earlier he had been selling junk, old iron, metals and rope down on the waterfront and living in Washington.) In the same year, 1875, the massive new Presbyterian Church, embellished with spires and turrets, was constructed on the opposite corner.[15] Gone forever was the pear orchard and the view of fields beyond up the hill to The Heights.

Two blocks further north, as a direct outgrowth of Henry D. Cooke's initiative, still another neighborhood was developing along the R Street summit. In 1868 when Q Street was opened up, the heirs of Martha Custis Peter, owner of Tudor Place, decided to sell the northern half of the estate, a highly desirable, well-placed parcel, consisting of 75,000 square feet with many splendid oaks and what amounted to first water rights on the flow from the High Service Reservoir. They engaged Philip H. Darneille, the popular realtor, to handle the subdivision and sale of lots. A compatible Virginian who after the war had moved to 1627 31st Street, across from Tudor Place, Darneille had married a granddaughter of Mrs. Rebecca Williams. About forty years old at the time, he would prove himself throughout the rest of the century the most able and successful agent among the many who gradually found Georgetown an attractive market for their talents. Cutting up the Peter piece into five lots of different sizes and prices (from $15 to $45 per square foot), he had sold the whole piece within two weeks of putting the place on the market.[16] Darneille also joined with Brooke Williams, who lived on R Street where the Home for the Blind is now, to sell portions of the latter's property. By 1878 nine substantial houses set in good yards, and built for the most part by businessmen commuting to Washington, lined upper 31st Street.

A few blocks south on the same street the forces that determine how a town develops were shifting and changing the life of an important block, the Post Office block. It had become one of the busiest in town.

In 1868 a "a consummation devoutly to be wished" had occurred when mail service was increased to daily deliveries from Washington. Although by New Year's Eve 1877 twenty-six postboxes had been installed about town,[17] there was as yet no carrier service, so people were coming and going to and from the Post Office all day long. (The street had a steep grade so runaway horses came and went with equal frequency.) Canal boatmen and hundreds of seafaring men found it a convenience to have

"Georgetown at a Standpoint"

Typical of the Georgetown housing boom in the 1870s is this house at 3121 O Street, built in 1874 by George Shoemaker, flour miller.

their mail directed here. Farmers from neighboring counties outside the District would pick up orders for the next week's market day. At Robert Fugitt's Post Office restaurant, people discovered oysters, and game in season was still a poor man's pleasure. Across the street a trio of dressmakers plied their fussy trade, and an immigrant from Hesse-Darmstadt made cigars and repaired guns and locks. In 1876 the six Cropley brothers bought the lot south of the alley and built a one-story brick office building, which was immediately rented to attorneys, physicians, architects, and civil engineers. Ten years later these professionals would move their offices to Washington. But in this decade their presence in the block contributed a new urban flavor.

All in all, the special Georgetown look, consisting of the juxtaposition of architectural styles and disparate rooflines, had its genesis in this volatile decade. Building permits are not on file until 1877, so that the records do not show whether such houses as 3314 and 3318 O Street or the imposing Libbey houses were built to an individual architect's specifications. But Georgetown builders on the whole resembled Adam Bede, George Eliot's idealistic yet impractical hero. "My notion," declared Adam, "is that a practical builder that's got a bit o' taste, makes the best architect for common things; and I've ten times the pleasure i' seein' after the work when I've made the plan myself." The builders worked from copy or pattern-books published in England, Philadelphia, Boston or New York, and with results sturdy enough to endure the abuse and caprice of individual owners through many decades to follow.

Although by the end of the 70s almost a quarter of statutory Georgetown remained to be developed and was still in the form of large private estates or undeveloped land in the northwest sector, a dwelling count in 1876 showed there were 1,111 dwellings of brick and 1,105 of frame construction.[18] The drop in the number of private stables, from 76 in 1876 to 42 ten years later, dramatically illustrates the loss of open space through the inevitable process of urbanization.[19] Riley A. Shinn, the perennial Irish optimist who had refurbished the old Union Hotel, regarded Georgetown's future through rose-colored glasses. "Yes, Sir," he exclaimed to the press. "In the past ten years we've built property amounting roughly

Georgetown Life, 1865-1900

to $250,000. Some call the old town a cemetery. But you just wait and see!"[20]

Longtime small businessmen saw the future with a more jaundiced eye. It was all very well, they argued, to see how crowded the inter-city streetcars were, to see traffic moving east and west in such numbers, and to see five thousand dollar houses built. But few newcomers could afford the rent of $700 to $1,000 a year. "There's a brisk demand for small houses of five to seven rooms, and those offered will be taken up immediately."[21]

Soon building associations formed along the established English pattern. They sold shares and, in proportion to his shares, a member could borrow to finance the construction of a row or a house.[22] These successful institutions added many new dwellings to the rental pool and helped attract newcomers to town.

But a deep-seated anxiety about being swallowed up by the growing capital city periodically turned Georgetowners into manic-depressives. It was typical that in July 1874 John McGill and others found the town so attractive they began boasting it could become a summer resort. Two months later, the reverse happened. At the entrance to town, on a triangle created by the intersection of M Street and Pennsylvania Avenue, the BPW had erected a picturesque fountain surrounded by a watering trough. "In the spring," editorialized John McGill, "it watered horses, small boys, and cattle driven into town from the east. Now it is a cistern. The history of Washington is onward and upward. Georgetown is at a standpoint. Its land values are going down. It is time to amalgamate."[23]

He struck an Achilles' Heel. In 1875 when the Commissioners first governed the District, the Assessor had inspected the Georgetown tax assessment books and declared the contents "chaotic." "Property would have to be assessed at less than one-third or one-half the amount of its cash value as estimated for commercial purposes on the market."[24] The results were appalling. Across the board former assessments were crossed out and new ones entered at much lower values depending on how accessible or inaccessible the BPW had left the property, its age, whether it abutted a depreciating neighborhood, or in the case of waterfront properties, whether the buildings were left above or below grade, and how far.[25]

Stung by this cavalier treatment, concerned citizens remembered the success of Georgetown's historic arch-rival, Alexandria, when in 1846 it won retrocession to Virginia. Burrowing into the records, they found that as a result Alexandria's population in the 50s grew 40%, while in the same decade Georgetown grew only by 400 persons or 5%. After retrocession, Congress allowed $20,000 for roads leading into Alexandria and not one cent for Georgetown.[26] So, aided by three prominent lawyers, each representing the Democratic, southern-oriented tradition Georgetown had always stood for, the merchants agreed to memorialize Congress once more for retrocession:

"Georgetown at a Standpoint"

> It is not in the interests of our people that they should remain tied to Washington City as mere feeders to the treasury of that centre of experiments...Maryland stands with open arms and loving heart to welcome her plucky son to her bosom again.[27]

The fact that Georgetown was the terminus of the C&O Canal, added weight to their argument.

If Congress even considered the petition, there is no record of it. Quite the contrary: On June 11, 1878, Congress enacted the Organic Act. From then on Georgetown was called West Washington. A painful discouraging period followed. Churches lost membership to Washington parishes.[28] The Adams Express Office and the ticket office of the Baltimore & Ohio Railroad were closed down.[29] Overnight a wag with a warped sense of humor hung the office with crepe and an explanatory placard bearing the ugly message: "Died of economy - no inquest necessary."[30] Severe epidemics of yellow fever and diphtheria broke out. The Kennebec Ice Company sold out. The economy declined. Total land values in the 595.8 acres dropped from $6,272,019 in 1874 to an all-time low of $4,013,888 in 1884.[31] (This was in sharp contrast to the concurrent rise in value of County real estate which in that year exceeded that of Georgetown for the first time. The County was all of the District north of the Georgetown and Washington city boundaries.) Despite the diverting sight of Joseph Birch's cow with her triplets grazing in his yard back of the coffin workshop on M Street, times were dull.[32]

X

The Ludlow Patton

The drawing on page 56, done in pen and watercolor on paper, presents a view of the Potomac River west of the Aqueduct Bridge. Measuring 24" × 19", it celebrates the successful launching in the spring of 1875 of the *Ludlow Patton*, a steam canal barge, on the Chesapeake & Ohio Canal. A carpenter's certificate accompanying the registration at the Port of Georgetown issued May 31, 1875, shows that the *Patton* weighed 60 20/100 tons and measured 86' × 14' × 5'.[1]

For some years the Canal Company had yearned for such a steam-powered, propellor-driven vessel to eliminate the need for mule-power and shorten the travel time on the 180-mile route between Cumberland and Georgetown. Several inventors had tried and failed. But at length, an ingenious young fellow about twenty-five years of age named Henry G. Wagner patented a propellor which the pilot could raise and lower at will to control the speed of the boat and thus the riffles of water in its wake. Excessive speed would cause a heavy wake and erode the banks of the canal. Wagner was a first generation American, whose parents had emigrated from Wiesbaden in the 1840s, and by trade a watch and clock maker with a shop at 3221 M Street. Evidently, while fixing clocks and watches, his mind was working out the engineering relationship between propellor and engine frame, boiler and hydraulic steam cylinder.

With his patent granted in April 1874, Wagner gave the green light to the boatyard in Cumberland to begin construction.[2] Six months later the *Patton* was brought down the canal to the Duvall Foundry at 30th Street where the boiler was installed amidships and the propellor and rudder apparatus attached to the stern. A pilot's wheel, a model of neatness and beauty and fashioned by a Georgetown cabinetmaker, was also attached. The coping was painted a gay and patriotic red, white and blue, and with the helmsman in his well and Old Glory waving proudly from the bow, the barge returned to Cumberland for its first load. Its maiden voyage with 109 tons of coal in the first week of June set a record of seventy-four hours between the two terminal points.[3]

At this time Wagner must have commissioned the unknown artist (who can be spotted in the lower right corner attended by a faithful Fido and painting with his left hand) to record the scene when the *Patton*, riding high in the water, was going toward Cumberland. The artist made a second drawing, now in the possession of Wagner's grandson who lives in

55

The Ludlow Patton

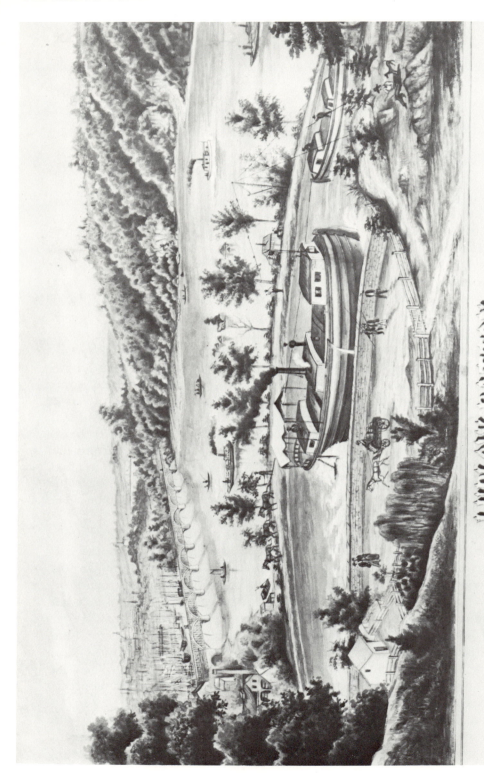

(From the collection of Edgar William and Bernice Chrysler Garbisch at the National Gallery of Art.)

56

Georgetown Life, 1865-1900

Georgetown, which is a continuation of the scene around to the north showing the Georgetown College buildings as well as the path of the canal into Georgetown. The *Patton*, now low in the water, is heading toward the coal docks. (This scene was used by the Junior League of Washington as the jacket for its valuable and handsome book called *The City of Washington: An Illustrated History*, published in 1977.)

During that initial summer the *Patton* made thirteen more roundtrips than any other barge, claiming to move one ton one mile for less than one-quarter of one cent and to have been free from repairs during the entire six-month season.[4] Indeed, its success encouraged the construction of five other steam boats at Cumberland, and Wagner himself made enough money to have two others built and launched in 1876.[5] Watching the craft carefully for signs of damage to the canal, the directors of the Company finally decided that serious damage did occur if the speed exceeded five miles per hour. Consequently, the vessels had to adhere to this limit.

Wagner's trio reigned supreme for four years, a cause for rejoicing among the many Georgetowners who held Canal Company stock, and for equally keen disappointment when the vessels disappeared from service four years later.[6] Why this occurred we do not know, although Wagner family legend has it that they burned beyond repair. But other steamers also gradually retired from the trade, apparently due to the frequent storms and floods battering the ill-fated waterway during the Eighties. Perhaps when he was drawing the scene, the anonymous artist had in mind Aesop's fable of the Tortoise and The Hare, for he carefully painted in the background, behind the *Patton*, a canal barge of the old-fashioned type, drawn by three mules aided by two laborers arduously poling the vessel on.

Who was Ludlow Patton and why name a boat for him? We can answer the first question, but must only speculate as to the second. Patton was a New York banker married to Abby Hutchinson of the Hutchinson Family Singing Group, famous in the antebellum era for their tours of the East Coast promoting abolition, Free Soil, and the civil rights of women and blacks. During the war and afterwards, they kept right on singing at inaugurations and funerals of noted figures, and even got as far west as Hutchinson, Minnesota, a town named for them. Patton was the advance man, making bookings and keeping accounts.[7]

Canalboat owners named their vessels for all kinds of odd reasons: to honor a C&O official, perhaps, or to celebrate a new baby or a sweetheart. One boat named *The Alaska* was launched right after the United States acquired that territory. Or an owner might simply pick an appealing name out of the newspaper, one which had the aplomb and style that he thought distinguished his boat. This is probably what young Wagner did. Certainly his grandson today was never given any reason to believe otherwise about this momentous event in the family annals.

The panoramic background of the drawing is rich in detail peculiar to the year 1875. To the extreme left, nearby, are the buildings of the former Henry Foxall Foundry. Behind, beyond the Aqueduct Bridge access road, is a "forest" of masts of schooners lying at anchor near the coal-loading docks and awaiting their turn to load the soft, black cargo brought down from the Cumberland region. Some vessels have their topsails loosely furled as if almost ready to take off. Among them one may imagine, for example, the schooner *O. D. Witherill* (launched at Bath, Maine in 1847), which brought ice to Georgetown from the Kennebec River. On its return voyage it would carry an equal amount of coal to various Yankee ports to fuel the blast furnaces and forges for smelting iron ore in that fast-growing manufacturing region. By 1885 commerce of this kind had become so successful that the schooners had doubled their cargo capacity, their length, and the number of their masts.

Beyond the harbor rises the dome of the Capitol and the towers of the Smithsonian Castle as well as the stub of the unfinished Washington Monument, flying an American flag. St. Elizabeth's Hospital is visible, slightly to the left of center, in the middle of uninhabited farmland.

Then, running diagonally across the left portion of the drawing, there is the Alexandria Aqueduct. Built in the 1830s, by 1840 it was a conduit for barges of the C&O Canal Company carrying coal to Alexandria. When the Civil War broke out in 1861, the federal government seized it so as to control the wooded heights on the Virginia side and build on them a cordon of forts to prevent any sudden Confederate threat to the capital. During the war it was a military highway. Afterwards, as we have seen, the government sold this battered span to three Alexandria businessmen who erected the dual-purpose superstructure portrayed in the picture and made it a toll bridge. Inside, the highway was converted into a timber water-trough to hold six feet of water, allowing fifteen feet of headroom, with a towpath for mules four and a half feet wide.[8] On top of this tunnel was laid a hard dirt road for vehicular traffic and pedestrians, who were charged exorbitant tolls for its use. Each crossing to Georgetown by a Virginia farmer bringing fresh produce cost him fifty cents. Cattle and livestock were five cents a head, and a wagon with two horses 25 cents.[9] These rates, set by Congress, forced farmers to take a longer way around into Washington via the Long Bridge (now the 14th Street Bridge) or the Chain Bridge, thus cutting out Georgetown. Local merchants felt so angry and frustrated by this at the outset that they exhorted the community to obstruct any efforts to repair the basic dilapidated structure in the hope that the government would eventually buy the bridge and make it toll free or put a railroad there.

The Aqueduct led directly into the wooded hillside depicted here in all the lush green verdure of spring. At this point in our chronicle, nature conservancy buffs can rejoice. In 1861, when the Union Army confiscated the area, all the trees had been felled, leaving three-foot stumps and the timber falling down-hill. Gradually, as the fortifications were built with the timber, only the stumps were left. By 1875, however, enough new growth had flourished to present the beautiful sight shown here.[10]

This spacious hillside belonged in 1861 to William Henry Ross whose farmhouse can be spotted on the top of the hill to the right. When he left for the duration of the war to live in France, he deeded his farm to his daughter Carolyn Lambden who, in 1869, sold it to the Rosslyn Development Corporation. It was by combining the last syllable of her given name with her maiden name that the name Rosslyn was derived.[11]

To the right of center, on the crest of the hillside, another Old Glory waves on a tall flagpole near a house which, on the original, much larger drawing, is clearly of sophisticated Federal architectural design and can be identified as the Custis-Lee Mansion, now known as Arlington House. In 1875 this famous property was in litigation. George Washington Parke Custis had inherited it from his grandmother, Martha Washington, and at his death it passed to his daughter Mrs. Robert E. Lee. After her death it became the property of her son Geroge Washington Custis Lee. In 1861 the federal government confiscated the 1,100 acres, and after 1864 began burying its dead there. Following his mother's death, Custis Lee worked singlehandedly to regain his disputed inheritance, first in the Circuit Court, finally in the Supreme Court. In 1879 the latter Court affirmed the former's decision, and he was compensated with a payment of $150,000.[12]

We cannot leave this charming piece of art, allocated by the National Gallery to the division of American Naive Painting, without pointing out a few features typical of the art produced by skilled, although largely untrained, amateurs of the period. Note the Three Sisters rocks painted behind the line of trees bordering the towpath. The horse and wagon carrying casks or barrels are heading for a stable or shed much too small to accommodate even the wagon, the horse appearing eager to get to his oats. Four steamboats show a rich black and polluting plume of smoke streaming behind indicating a strong west wind. Yet two of them indicate the wind blows from the east, while the three American flags suggest a strong breeze from the west. Whatever the idiosyncracies of the unknown artist-draftsman, we can only be thankful to him and to Henry G. Wagner for this lively record of an important event in local history.

XI

Newcomers - Male

Among the eleven hundred white newcomers living in Georgetown in 1880 who do not appear in the 1870 *City Directory*, the largest group was that of the federal clerks. In antebellum days seventy government employees lived here, and all were native Americans. After war was declared in April 1861, thirty-seven left for the Confederacy, never to return. Afterwards, the numbers increased dramatically, from 120 in 1870 to some 500 by 1900, a figure including 133 women (to whom the next chapter will be devoted).[1] In 1870 most clerks were transients, about a third living west of Wisconsin Avenue and the rest east of that crowded artery.

Ten years later, though, Georgetown had grown much more attractive as a place to settle. Two street railways tied it to Washington and the federal departments. In addition, for those who passed muster with the Georgetown Assembly, and many did, a lively social life animated the entire year. In winter the Assembly held balls and cotillions. In spring and fall there were boat races and picnics up to the Three Sisters, outings to the unusually accessible countryside, and all manner of cycling, tennis, boating, and even velocipede clubs, to join.

Local townsmen began to turn spare rooms into boarding facilities, convert their own domiciles into boarding houses, or build ells onto their houses to accommodate a relative or friend of a friend who had found a post. Building associations urged all local masons to build as fast as possible the low-rental housing they knew would attract more newcomers. By 1880 some three hundred new clerks began to strain the local housing potential, with one-third settling permanently in Georgetown.

These people were generally in their middle years and came, for the most part, from Ohio, New York, Pennsylvania, and Massachusetts, as well as, of course, from Virginia and Maryland. A few wandered up from North and South Carolina. Twenty-eight could be counted as immigrants from Europe and Britain. The majority worked in the usual federal departments, principally the Treasury because the horse-cars passed directly by that building. But ten at least, brilliant men all of them, used their special talents in the United States Naval Observatory, which until 1889 was on a promontory just across Rock Creek at 23rd to 25th and E Streets. By 1893 the new Naval Observatory at 34th and Massachusetts was completed, and they either walked or rode up to this site.

Georgetown Life, 1865-1900

During the last fifteen years of the century the quality of government clerks improved substantially, contributing yeasty dimensions to Georgetown society. Until the Chester Arthur administration, 1881-1885, the general fitness of most government workers was dubious. An applicant—of the right political party—had only to demonstrate he could write an ordinary business letter in a clear round hand, knew arithmetic and a smattering of accounting, and was bullheaded enough to confront the chief executive before breakfast in the latter's private suite, demanding a job. But in 1883, two years after President Garfield was assassinated by a crazed office-seeker, the immensely important Pendleton Act was passed, transforming what some called the "Snivel Service" into the Civil Service by eliminating the pervasive spoils system for most appointments and substituting one based on competitive merit.

The presence of more educated and competent federal clerks gave Georgetown prestige and restored its social desirability as a place to live. Although many newcomers moved three, four, or even five times, eventually they settled down, particularly those men who were in the higher ranks (many living in Georgetown earned as much as $4,000, a top salary for those days) and those whose positions transcended political change. Some even bought a lot in Oak Hill Cemetery, the ultimate test.

In addition to civil servants, by the 1890s many others coming to Washington were choosing Georgetown as the place to live—including men associated with the Smithsonian Institution, such as geologists, explorers, inventors, entomologists, astronomers and mathematicians; congressional librarians; and high-ranking service officers and their retired counterparts.[2] The Georgetown of the Nineties already was foreshadowing the sophisticated mix which characterizes it today.

Who were some of these newcomers? Dr. John Shaw Billings and his wife Catherine, who built 3027 N Street in 1874, would have been outstanding anywhere and became leaders in local society. Dr. Billings arrived as a surgeon in 1862. From his experience in many battles during the Civil War he had noted how fast wounds would heal when exposed to the open air. This observation on the merits of good ventilation in a hospital later contributed to his becoming the principal designing engineer for the Johns Hopkins Hospital in Baltimore. For thirty years he was the Army's medical statistician, and he served as chief of the Vital Statistics section of the 1880 census.[3]

While in charge of this part of the Tenth Census, he met another civil servant, a census clerk and engineer who later resided in Georgetown until his death in 1929 and whose family still owns the house he built in 1911 at 1617 29th Street. Virginia Hollerith says it was chicken salad that brought her father, Herman Hollerith, and Dr. Billings together. This son of a German immigrant from the Rhenish Palatinate came to live in Georgetown in 1879. A sociable fellow who liked athletics, he joined the Potomac Boat Club. At a Saturday evening club "social" he met one of Dr. Billings' daughters serving the salad. She noticed him smacking his

Newcomers - Male

1525 35th Street was the home of Alexander Melville Bell.

lips over it and suggested he ought to taste some of her mother's salad. Soon the invitation arrived, and the two statisticians met.

Dr. Billings is then said to have taken the younger clerk through a room at the Division of Vital Statistics, where hundreds of clerks were bent over tables laboriously hand-tallying long lists of figures. "Hollerith," he said, 'there ought to be some mechanical way of doing that job, something on the principle of the French Jaquard loom, whereby holes on a card regulate the pattern.''

Hollerith remembered this, and so it was that he undertook the first crude experiments leading to the invention of the tabulating card. Taking a train one day, he noted that when the conductor first took his ticket, he punched out a description of the ticket-holder—light hair, dark eyes, large nose, etc. This gave Hollerith the idea of making a punch photograph of each person to be tabulated, and eventually led to patents that became the basis for the IBM computer.[4]

By 1893 Hollerith had set up his laboratory at 1054 31st Street (where Canal Square shopping mall now is located), and during his lifetime in Georgetown, before and after his marriage to a local girl, Lucia Talcott, he lived in five different places around town.[5] Governments in Italy, Switzerland and Russia bought his machines, and they were successfully used in the Eleventh Census. His brilliant career made him a millionaire.

Dr. Asaph Hall, a powerful magnet for astronomers and nautical scientists, the most distinguished in the $4,000 class, was another Georgetowner of international renown. He discovered the satellites of the planet Mars and lived for thirty years at 2715 N Street.[6]

Another outstanding newcomer was George Casilear who came from New York City in 1862 as an engraver at the Bureau of Engraving and Printing and lived for over thirty years at 3019 N. He knew all about banknote engraving, particularly the process of grooving a plate with fine, wavey, hairlike lines to defeat counterfeiters, and presided over a corps of the finest engravers in the nation. To perfect a single plate there had to be men with a genius for landscape, human portraits, animal portraits, and lettering ornamentation. He picked or trained them all, in the process becoming another $4,000 man. During his long residence on N Street he attracted other printers and mapmakers, some from England and France and even the French colonies of the West Indies, to live nearby in rental housing at the corners of Dumbarton and 30th.[7]

Other foreigners settled in Georgetown too, among whom the most distinguished for almost half a century was Raphael Principe Thian, a Frenchman who became Chief Clerk of the Adjutant General's office of the War Department. Born in St. Denis, France, in 1830, he emigrated to Buffalo, then moved to New York in 1850. After spending the war years there in General Winfield Scott's office, he came to Washington. His well-disciplined, encyclopedic mind later turned out an amazing number of documents for the War Department on topics ranging from a history of the Confederate Flag and Seal to a legislative history of the line of the U.S. Army from 1775 to 1901. Between 1861 until 1912 when he died, he occupied or owned several prominent houses.[8]

Asaph Hall, 1829-1907, was an astronomer who, in 1877, discovered one of the two satellites of Mars whose orbits he had calculated. He was born in Goshen, Conn., and in 1863 was appointed to the U.S. Naval Observatory. He retired in 1891 and returned to New England. (Courtesy, U.S. Naval Observatory)

The roster of civil servants who became longtime residents here was sprinkled with people like those described above. But not all of the newcomers were federal clerks. Some were businessmen in insurance, banking and construction, or lawyers, physicians and other professionals. Among these were several architects who worked for the Treasury and were responsible—in those days before the General Services Administration—for furnishing and rendering useful the constantly increasing number of federal offices and buildings. Franklin Steele, a real estate figure, after twenty years on the Minnesota frontier, came with his large family to buy Prospect House at 3508 Prospect Avenue so as to give his children proper educations and an introduction to an established society.[9] Archibald Roane, of a famous old Tennessee family with roots in Virginia, first came so that his sons could clerk in the Senate and get a taste of government.[10] Still another Southerner, a great nephew of John Marshall and a collateral descendant of Francis Scott Key, Judge John J. Key of Kentucky, bought 3327 P Street for his retirement.[11] Also in this senior citizen group were Alexander Melville Bell and his brother David from Bran-

Newcomers - Male

Herman Hollerith (1860-1929) in the late 1880s. Hollerith filed his first patent for the punched tabulating card in 1887. He met his future wife, Lucia Talcott, a member of an established Georgetown family, at one of the Georgetown Assemblies.

ford, Ontario, uncles of Alexander Graham Bell. The inventor was living near Dupont Circle while solidifying his patents on the telephone, and his long-legged figure was a daily sight in Georgetown as he walked out P or Q Street to visit his relatives.

Already in the 1880s and 1890s, therefore, a wide-ranging geographical and intellectual spectrum was beginning to distinguish Georgetown society. And the infusion of newcomers greatly enriched Georgetown's architectural heritage, even if no one recognized it as such in those days. The magnitude of the inflow is revealed by the fact that of 4,104 names of heads of household in the Georgetown directory for 1901, only some four hundred had appeared a generation earlier in the 1870 *Washington & Georgetown City Directory*. Many newcomers were, of course, transients and, as the economic scene shifted or administrations changed, would move away. But due to well-established schools and churches and the way the local community supplied domestic shopping needs, as well as to the variety of residential options, many more stayed and maintained the housing base which has been so important in attracting and accommodating the thousands who today make Georgetown so popular an address.

XII

Teapots on the Windowsills

In 1861 a group of women invaded the hitherto completely male-dominated sphere of the United States Government. At the outset, none was a Georgetowner. But by 1870, eight of the 120 federal clerks living in Georgetown were female, and thirty years later, with some 500 clerks residing here, 133 were women. Thirty of them came from such well-known local families as the Clagetts, Buckeys, Cassins, Addisons, Cropleys, Magruders, and Talcotts. Not only had working for the government lost its social stigma but, more important, a social change of immeasurable proportions had begun. Georgetown women were among its early protagonists.

After the Union Army's first crushing defeat, at the Battle of Bull Run in July 1861, President Abraham Lincoln called for half a million volunteers to create an army. It became clear that the war would be much longer than originally predicted, and the U. S. Treasurer, General Francis Spinner, otherwise known as Father Spinner because of his crusty yet avuncular ways, grew anxious. Monthly expenditures of no less than twenty million dollars confronted him, and Treasury cash deposits stood at zero. To meet the payroll, Congress passed the Legal Tender Act authorizing paper money to be printed, and these original "greenbacks" were first issued in August 1861.

Production of this issue meant printing large sheets each containing several notes, with blank spaces for the signatures of the U. S. Treasurer and the Registrar. Working under great pressure to cut and trim the sheets, the twenty male clerks assigned to the job found themselves cutting their fingers, getting blistered thumbs and spotting their clothes and the notes with blood.[1] A practical, sixty-year old fellow with three daughters, Father Spinner knew what women could do with shears. Approaching Salmon P. Chase, Secretary of the Treasury, he suggested hiring a few women as temporaries to do the job. Already for a decade at least, women had been doing work for the General Land Office copying land warrants at home, even though technically it was done in the name of some male relative. Given this attitude toward women doing men's work, the Secretary balked. Spinner then added that women could do the job cheaper. This changed the matter, and Chase agreed to the experiment. Later, he admitted the initiative had been a success, and from then on women were permanent fixtures on the Treasury payroll at $600 a year, compared to $1,200 paid the men.[2]

Teapots on the Windowsills

Many years later a longtime Treasury clerk reminisced for an *Evening Star* reporter about those first weeks with the women. About a dozen women, mostly unmarried, sat along both sides of a long table, a stack of note-sheets in front of each one, shears in hand, nimbly cutting through the units (later a device like a guillotine was used), then trimming the edges and passing each note to the men at the head of the table to sign and stack for shipping. In too much of a hurry to call in the U. S. Treasurer and the Registrar, they forged the signatures. That autumn sixty million dollars in paper notes were issued. Congress then voted another issue, and the same assembly line, this time augmented by three times as many women, turned out the money.[3]

What was remarkable about this new venture was not merely the employment of women. Women after all had long been earning money in the marketplace. In 1860 in Georgetown, for example, you could find women employed as milliners, dressmakers, boardinghouse keepers, and saloon and "eating" saloon owners. Women ran junk shops and bookstores, sold furniture, fancy goods or notions, acted as midwives, were tobacconists, and embalmed flowers for funerals. They taught art and music in the public schools or ran a private elementary academy. One even was a post mistress for several years. Some of these jobs were executed by immigrants who had done the same sort of thing in the old country. But the women at the Treasury in the 1860s were not immigrants. They were native white Americans of the middle or upper class, the daughters, wives and widows of doctors, lawyers, ministers, and other

These prints appeared in Ten Years in Washington *by Mary Clemmer Ames, published in Hartford in 1874.*

Georgetown Life, 1865-1900

federal clerks, and they had had a secondary education.[4]

So their employment must be recognized for the bold, courageous step it was. Here, for the first time, a woman was leaving a familiar environment for the uncertainties and agitations attending work elbow-to-elbow with strange men. And it was literally elbow-to-elbow. Contemporary engravings of women at work in the Treasury show cramped assembly lines, with women standing next to men, or even bending over tubs of ink in the printing office. The job, moreover, was carried out in the unaccustomed rigor of an office, six days a week for a set segment of time.

These women had to have something to bridge their physical separation from home and provide comfort during a fatiguing and alien day. Thus it was no wonder that, in an age when there were no African violets to hover over, teapots soon invaded every windowsill. But it was not teapots which, as early as 1866, led to threats to discharge all lady clerks. It was flirtations. Indeed by 1869 they had become so objectionable and distracting that some disgruntled officials were calling women clerks "treasury courtesans."[5]

Some women were almost ready to abandon their jobs too. They found it offensive to lift their skirts every time they encountered a spittoon, especially the one at the bottom of the Treasury stairwell. Men had refused to have it moved because hitting this bull's eye from five floors up constituted a special and diverting challenge.

Throughout the war the shortage of men available for employment remained critical, however, so the teapots remained in place until shortly after Lincoln's assassination. Then Secretary Chase's successor, Andrew

Teapots on the Windowsills

McCullough, who had long been the Comptroller of the Currency and, ever since the new paper money was issued, had passed daily through the workrooms, issued a directive banishing all domestic containers brought from home to the offices where women were employed. Thereafter line drawings of Treasury offices in contemporary magazines show only a stern bare room, with women sitting stiffly upright on the folds of their heavy skirts, looking straight down at their work. It was a grim environment, no doubt about it.

Yet throughout this period, and until 1880 when the Bureau of Engraving and Printing moved to a site near the Washington Monument, many women were employed in the Bureau's intricate and messy processes, and particularly those from Georgetown since the Washington & Georgetown horse-drawn trolley passing along Pennsylvania Avenue stopped at the Treasury. Some employees had an especially disagreeable experience. Their job was done in the vast coal bins of the Treasury basement, with coal stacked at one end and the manufacturing processes at the other. Later the work was transferred but the transfer brought no improvement at all. The women left a murky, grimy situation for one in the attic of the Treasury where in winter the heat scarcely ever reached any helpful intensity and in summer the ceilings got so hot they had to cover their heads with brown paper to keep from getting scalded.[6]

In the workrooms on the intermediate floors, a constant irritation was irregular ventilation. In 1889 one clerk named Frances Wadleigh recalled that disputes among the employees about drafts from open windows erupted frequently. "The air was foul and unpleasant, and we all considered it unhealthy, particularly when we grew so cramped for space we had to sit close to the windows with little room between us and the next table or rank of employees."[7]

By the Seventies the administration had seen fit to separate the sexes into jobs supposed to be compatible with their abilities. Women became copyists and counters of money old and new, prepared burnt and partially destroyed notes for redemption, and proved themselves much faster than men in detecting counterfeits. Thus it was especially galling to the more intelligent and skillful women to observe the hundreds of drones in the Treasury hive in Classes 1 or 2, the highest paid classes, receiving $1,200 or $1,600 or more annually, almost twice what women earned, when even the supervisors recognized the latter's superior performance. "Among the men," one observer wrote, "many were studying law, medicine, or divinity, and only using the government position as a stepping stone to something better. Artists too, and musicians, even elocutionists and actors, have all graduated from Uncle Sam's employ."[8]

During this period federal departments in Washington altogether employed about 650 women although few had any career ambitions. They simply needed money, or had no home and had to earn to have one.[9] There was, for example, Emma R. Graves, born in New York State, who came to Georgetown in 1864 at age 18 to live with her sister, Mrs. John

Georgetown Life, 1865-1900

Joyce. She had lost her mother long before, her father and two brothers died during the war, and she had no other place to go. Entering the Treasury as a counter at $900 a year, she worked as such until 1900 before she was promoted to the next class earning $1,000. She remained at this level as late as 1919. Her brother-in-law, Colonel Joyce, called himself a poet, but probably drew a pension or lived off some other mysterious resource. The Joyces lived at 3238 R Street, now called "The Little Red House," a commodious and probably very expensive house to maintain. Undoubtedly, the Joyces appreciated Emma's contribution to their budget.

Emma obtained her place due to fulfilling the major requirements asked of female applicants for federal posts in those years. She had excellent political patronage ties. She was educated. She was financially needy.[10] Her sponsor was the Hon. Preston King, a politician from Ogdensburg, New York, who had entered Congress in 1845 as a Free Soiler, became Senator, and as a strong Union man, later Chairman of the National Republican Party. Emma approached him just in time. An excessively conscientious man he grew so harrassed by the invasion of office-seekers and a fear of failure to perform properly as Chairman, that on November 13, 1865, he tied a bag of shot to his body and jumped off the Hoboken ferry crossing the Hudson River at New York City.[11]

In addition to proving her financial need and ability to muster patronage, Emma had to pass a Civil Service examination. She survived this ordeal, but many women became so agitated by the prospect of taking it, that they would settle for the Broom Brigade which got out the mops and pails after 3 p.m. daily when the Treasury began to empty.

Once in a clerical job, a woman's difficulties mounted. The major one was the fear or the actuality of sexual harassment. So-called "good" women found themselves continually under suspicion, or imagined that they were. To illustrate this theme, a bit of verse was written in 1871 by George Allen Townsend, editor of a Washington weekly, the *Washington Capital*.

> No prude is she, to seek and pry
>   If each one round her be a saint;
>
> She knows her own soul pure and high
>   And nothing else can do her taint.
>
> She knows that dear temptations vex
>   This weak and craving human nature
>
> And how the mighty spell of sex
>   O'ercomes a lonely, loving woman.
>
> Her intuition teaches that
>   The statesman still is but a sinner
>
> And Mammon drops his key to chat
>   As readily as General Spinner.[12]

Teapots on the Windowsills

Women correspondents from distant states loved to find a juicy tale to relay back home. Cindy Sondik Aron, who studied the early women clerks in depth, tells how Mrs. E. N. Chapin from Marshallton, Iowa, author of a book called *American Court Gossip*, informed the readers of the *Iowa State Register* about a Mrs. John Smith, widow, who had journeyed to Washington to inquire about her husband's pension. Finding the proceedings delayed, and with two children to support, Mrs. Smith approached a senator and requested assistance in obtaining a post in a department. Apparently, the senator responded with an offensive proposition, at which the plucky widow seized the inkstand from the table, dashed its contents against his fine coat and shirtfront, and made for the door like an angry deer, only to find it locked. The senator, regaining his composure, informed Mrs. Smith that he was only testing her "to see if you were a proper person to put into so responsible a position," and immediately authorized her appointment.[13]

Much more agitating than the chance of being compromised were the complex elements in the total office atmosphere. Male employees made insulting remarks. One man, who said that "it made no difference to him whether a woman was a harlot or a virgin as long as she did the work," was reported to have "made women sit on his desk or at his feet, and allowed messengers to walk about with hats on their heads and whistling at us." These attitudes made some women clash with the supervisor who, in one instance, ordered a defiant clerk to turn her desk so she had to look at the wall.[14]

Despite all the complaints, however, many plusses could be found and, in retrospect, were recognized as such by the clerks themselves. Mrs. Aron describes how they enjoyed an esprit de corps. There were collections for weddings and funerals and for helping each other by contributing toward a brother's college education or meeting the grocery bill in a family of ten.[15] The women also took pride in the evident impact on office administration and behavior their presence had caused. By 1880 signs were posted prohibiting smoking in halls or in any room occupied by ladies. (This prohibition did not include spitting, however!) Standards of male behavior improved and brought men to their feet when women entered the room.

Above all, women found confidence in their ability to support a family, compete in the examinations, and confront a strange man to ask for a position. Many developed skills they had no idea they had, and found self-esteem in copying when they did it well and were praised for it. Officials were more surprised than disappointed that women were not the docile workers they had expected and that, given the right job, they could perform better than men. Women found that traditional standards of female behavior were growing fuzzy and losing validity. They moved about Washington on the trolleys, entered dancing classes, went on picnics and excursions with men to whom they had not been properly introduced, and discovered that they could converse easily, even form a friendship, without feeling they had taken that dreaded first step on the road to ruin.

Thus, though they would never know the outcome of their initiatives, this pioneer group did carve out a new type of person from which it was natural for the many developments of the future to evolve. Nineteenth century femininity was beginning to grow passé.

XIII

From Niederseebach to M Street

Most of the newcomers who chose Georgetown after the Civil War did so because it was near Washington. But there were others who did not come simply to be near the capital's job market. Many of these were immigrants who were drawn to the town's pleasant neighborhood personality and to the broad river and the countryside so accessible for family outings. Some had lived first elsewhere in the United States and may have found the social system too rigid for them to break through and advance. Now they searched a felicitous climate in which to live and find openings to exercise their native talents, to make a new beginning.

Georgetown's rapidly increasing population offered great opportunities for new businesses. By 1880, in fact, only 20 of the 130 shopkeepers on both sides of Wisconsin Avenue had been there twenty years earlier.

Before the war and for some time afterwards, Wisconsin Avenue must have been a quiet, pleasant street, a place to stroll and gossip and for children to play, despite roaming livestock, horse droppings and the myriad flies endemic to the horse-drawn era. But by the Eighties traffic along this corridor leading north to a fast developing County, and beyond that, a farming countryside, had increased. Traversing it became so precarious that to satisfy their divided clientele, grocers would open shops on opposite corners, and so did restaurants, oyster bars, and saloons. Shoe and boot-fitters, apothecaries, small dry goods stores and tailors, even dairy product stores, faced each other across the street.

Several industrious foreigners were working out successful careers. Joseph Schladt, a native of Prussia who emigrated in 1860, had learned bartending in Washington. At 1216 Wisconsin Avenue, in a building long called The Carriage House, he ran what amounted to a German gasthaus with German and Swiss boarders enjoying his yellow lager, sausage, and dumplings.

Another immigrant started a pie-baking company at the corner where Peoples Drug Store now stands. Born in the West Indies and emigrating in 1847, Henry Copperthite lived in Connecticut until 1885. Then moving to Georgetown, he collected four other bakers working independently in the same block and reactivated the Connecticut Pie Company. It

Georgetown Life, 1865-1900

The Connecticut Pie Company on the corner where the People's Drug Store is now. The wagons face across O Street, and the tracks belong to the Georgetown-Tenallytown Rail Road running up Wisconsin Avenue.

delivered fruit and custard pies and decorated cakes to and for customers from upper Georgetown until just before World War I.

A broom factory at 3322 Volta Place nearby was also a new enterprise. Why George Fritch, who emigrated from Wurtemberg in 1850 and spent twenty years in New York before coming south, selected Georgetown can only be a speculation. He didn't arrive until the Board of Public Works had cut its swathe and the Metropolitan Railroad had laid tracks and begun to run its horsecars on P Street. So he may well have hunted for the dirtiest small town he could find which needed the sweep of a strong German broom!

His location was about the most unpleasant, olfactorily speaking, in Georgetown. It stood opposite the hundreds of desecrated graves of the old Presbyterian Cemetery, whose brick walls had been vandalized and gravestones toppled, where vines and creepers made a thicket, and the burial vault remained unopened for long periods. All through the rest of the century this noisome wilderness was the subject of popular, even angry, complaints to the D.C. Commissioners. Yet nearby at 1507 33rd Street George Fritch bought a house and made it his home and that of his sons and grandsons for almost forty years.

His initiative paid off. Employing nine men at $1 a day and working

Niederseebach to M Street

3301 Volta Place. In the late 19th centry the Twenty Buildings (built around 1820) extended from 33rd up to 34th Street on Volta Place. In 1907 all except these two structures were demolished to get rid of the Presbyterian Cemetery and make room for a park, now the Volta Playground. George Fritch's broom factory was across the street for about thirty years.

them, as well as himself and his widowed son and grandsons, from sunup to sundown, in 1880 he netted $2,000 a year after paying out $1,000 in wages and $3,000 for materials. In 1914 the Fritch family was still living at 1507 33rd, marketing brooms.[1]

A current pun identified the most unusual and successful German immigrants. Riley Shinn's bottling establishment, which turned out stout, ale, and porter, was a longtime prosperous business on Olive Street. Somebody asked: Why is Shinn's like the City of Jerusalem? The answer: Because Hebrews drink there.[2] By 1850 some fifty thousand German Jews from the Rhineland, Alsace, and Bavaria had found a kinder destiny in the United States.[3] Well-educated and fluent in French and German as well as Hebrew, forty or more merchants had trickled into Georgetown, most of German or French origin and all Reformists escaping the rigid restrictions imposed by their native governments. During the war many stores along M Street had been vacated between 29th Street and the market space at Potomac Street, and by 1865 had an entirely new set of proprietors, German and German Jewish. A clannish lot, Prussians settled next to Prussians, Bavarians next to Bavarians. As women shopped along the street, basket in one hand, one or two children dragging at the other, almost more German was heard than English, with a good bit of Hebrew mixed in. Still a third group settled

Georgetown Life, 1865-1900

west of the Farmers & Mechanics Bank in the 3100 block of M Street.

Among the newcomers were two brothers, Wolf and Bernard Nordlinger, and their relatives, whose descendants are outstanding in the Washington Jewish community today. In overall pattern their stories resemble those of most immigrants of that era. Born in Alsace, Wolf, the elder by six years, emigrated in 1853 through the lower Rhine district on a Georgia-bound vessel which took him to Savannah. The Rhine was a major emigrant route. Navigable from Basel, Switzerland, it joined the Main and Neckar rivers flowing through Hesse, Bavaria, and Wurtemberg, to form a route tapping all regions of German migration.[3] The route also tapped Alsace where a new industry was developing—the manufacture of cloth from raw cotton. Ships from the southern United States would carry cotton to the lower Rhineland, then return with emigrants whose first glimpse of the United States was often New Orleans or Savannah. Wolf Nordlinger labored eleven long, hard years in the antebellum countryside of the future Confederacy before reaching Georgetown in 1864 with his wife Sarah and their two Georgia-born children.

While little is known of Wolf's pre-Georgetown life, we know a great deal more about his younger brother Bernard.*

Family tradition and valuable personal documents provide vivid clues to the profile of this "Confederate Soldier and Unofficial Rabbi," as his grandson describes him.

> A passport was issued to him [wrote his grandson] on April 28, 1858, in Strasbourg, then part of the French empire. He was a native of Niederseebach, France. According to the age of the emigrant recorded in the passport - given as 27 - he was born in 1831. From the passport it appears that his height was one meter, 62 centimeters, which I calculate to be 63.8 inches, or somewhat in excess of five foot, three inches, obviously a small man.
>
> Family tradition indicates that before he emigrated, he had served in the army of Louis Napoleon during the Crimean War, serving at the siege of Sebastopol. The record establishing the truth of the latter statement is a copy of a letter addressed to the French Minister of War dated May 24, 1904, an inquiry relating to a possible pension to be granted to French veterans. It contains the following paragraph:
>
>> One Bernard Nordlinger, formerly a native of Niederseebach, in the province of Sou-Bar, France and now a resident of this city (Georgetown, D.C.) was enrolled in the spring of 1854 as a private under Louis Napoleon the Third, and served three years and three

---
* Bernard Isaac Nordlinger, a successful Washington lawer today, has written his grandfather's story for *The Record*, published by the Jewish Historical Society of Greater Washington in December 1971.

Niederseebach to M Street

months throughout the Crimean War, and was honorably discharged in the summer of 1857 at Cannes, France.

My father told me that my grandfather had entered the port of Savannah and became a peddler in 1858. He later settled in Macon, Georgia, where family documents and research of myself and others indicate he in fact did serve in a religious capacity in the Jewish congregation there. Later he served in the Confederate Army, was wounded in the second Battle of Bull Run, taken to the hospital in Washington where he recovered and then removed to Camp Parole near Annapolis. At the conclusion of the war, he returned to Washington where he settled in Georgetown, opening a shoe store on M Street.[5]

Since his brother Wolf was already established as a clothier at 3103 M Street, Bernard moved into the building across the street to sell shoes. Soon he married Hannah Rice, a native of Heidelberg. By 1875 they had three children, the first of whom was Isaac B. Nordlinger who for most of his life carried on the shoe business. He was the present Bernard I. Nordlinger's father.

Meanwhile, a cousin, Benoit Baer, from Alsace, one of the few immigrants to come directly to Georgetown, had set up a clothing house at 3128 M Street that became a nucleus around which other immigrants from Baden and Bavaria settled as clothiers. The Baer and Nordlinger buildings stand today, each with the family name carved into the pediment. The Baer building has five elaborate Roman revival columns with Corinthian capitals, and the Nordlinger building at 3130 has a broken pediment with an Adam-style vase in the center. The letters of the name are visible stretching across the width under four arched windows.

By the early Nineties the Nordlingers were no longer living over their shops, but had bought or built their own homes. Bernard's was at 3113 N Street. The present Bernard recalls that twelve people lived there, with only one bathroom in the house; the one in

Bernard Nordlinger, 1831-1908, French by birth and later a Confederate soldier and unofficial rabbi.

Georgetown Life, 1865-1900

the yard was for the maids. "It was amazing, though, how well it worked; we didn't get in each other's way." Wolf's house, which he built in 1882, was at 3032 N Street. Both families continued through the second and third generations in the family homes, and while some of the sons like Isaac W. Nordlinger, a son of Wolf, entered the practice of law, there was always one who operated the family business, whether clothing or shoes. The unusual fact that all Nordlingers owned their homes and stores free of mortgage further testifies to their solidity in the town well into the twentieth century.[6]

Later, Orthodox Jews from Lithuania, Latvia, and the Russian border provinces came to augment the community. They founded the Kesher Israel Congregation, and about 1911 built a synagogue at 2801 N Street, which today still has a very active congregation.

In many other American towns the mail order catalogue and chain store had arrived or were just around the corner. But without a railroad terminal until 1911, Georgetown families had to depend on local merchants to fill their needs. The Jewish shopkeepers provided much of what was needed, reinforcing the traditional concept of a downtown where residents could walk to and from their homes to shop. Additional trade came from the personnel of the Chesapeake & Ohio Canal Company, to whom scrip was issued by the Company for wages, redeemable and accepted by Georgetown merchants at face value.[7] The busy commerce on the Canal did not cease until about the time of World War I.

In these ways local trade remained healthy well after 1900. J. Bernard Wyckoff, who moved to Georgetown in 1922, remembers that even then people told him: "Buy your meats at Scheele's, ice creams at Stohlmann's, and shoes at Nordlinger's."

Maintaining the commercial fabric of Georgetown into the Twenties was an important contribution to making possible its residential rebirth in the Thirties and during and after the Second World War.

XIV

"An Immense Vessel"

On August 2, 1880, anyone watching the Potomac River opposite the stub of the unfinished Washington Monument would have been treated to a startling and awesome sight. Rounding Analostan Island came some diminutive steamtugs hauling and pushing upstream to Borden's Wharf in Georgetown the first four-masted schooner ever built, the *William L. White*.[1] Sails were furled; but at the top of each mast flew the house flags and from the aft spanker, Old Glory waved a salute. Built by a coal merchant from Taunton, Massachusetts, she was on her maiden voyage from Bath, Maine, with a cargo of 1,341 tons of pure Kennebec River ice. During the Seventies many other schooners with no more than two masts and only half the *White*'s capacity had put in at Borden's. But this vessel, 307' from after-part to jib boom, dwarfed them all. After launching at Bath, she had been hauled up the Kennebec to Gardiner to collect the ice, and then made the passage south to Georgetown in a record seven days.[2]

An oil painting of the William L. White, courtesy, Bath Marine Museum, Bath, Maine. The schooner's history was glorious but brief. On November 19, 1882, at 1 a.m. she was in collision with the S.S. Algiers and sank in six minutes off Five Fathom Rock, sixteen miles from Cape May, near the mouth of the Delaware River.

Georgetown Life, 1865-1900

With the cargo finally unloaded, Captain Babbitt, 6' tall and a regular old tar, invited the public aboard. All day people streamed through the vessel. They gawked and craned their necks to look up the arrow-straight masts, each 95' tall and 28" in diameter, made of Oregon red wood pine, and entirely free of knots or blemishes. They heard the Captain describe how each mast was rigged with a boom and a gaff to carry the 5,021 yards of duck comprising the sails. The anchor itself weighed 3,100 pounds, and to assist in turning the *White* in harbor, there were two kedges, one of 2,500 pounds and the other of 1,500. A donkey engine of 10 horsepower was used in hoisting sail and anchor, in loading and discharging cargo, and in pumping water. By using this engine, he had only required five men as crew. The living accommodations were excellent. The kitchen, pantry and dining room had high ceilings, and all furniture, the saloon cabins, and the staterooms were finished in walnut. The cost was $45,000.[3]

Georgetown's pride was boundless. The weather was beautiful. The canal flowed with enough water for the mills and the coal-laden canalboats. The coal unions did not strike. Merchants found nothing to grumble at. On August 10, as this specimen of the best timber, engineering, and commercial architecture of her day cleared for New Bedford with 1,470 tons of coal, crowds cheered her off.[4] A new era for Georgetown had arrived.

For the next thirty years the old port would play a major role in a dynamic economic development on the eastern seaboard. Since the Hudson River and the Berkshires were still insurmountable barriers to large-scale movement of coal by rail into New England, transportation by sea became the only solution.[5] The roundtrip concept of a single sea-carrier bringing ice from Maine to Washington and returning to New England with coal didn't take hold until the population demanded ice. In addition, the factory towns of New England had to discover the virtues of the soft, low-volatile, bituminous coal from the Appalachians. Used in blast furnaces and forges for smelting iron ore, this kind of coal was also preferred in the manufacture of paving which, with the construction of roads escalating everywhere, was in increased demand.

Simultaneously, with the growth of Washington and Baltimore, ice, an article considered a luxury ten or fifteen years earlier, now had become a necessity. The local D.C. market for ice, for example, amounted to 125,000 tons a year in the early Eighties. When an ice famine threatened just before the *White* arrived, the big consumers—the local brewers, butchers, fish and meat dealers, ice cream dealers, dairies, and restaurants—panicked. They even considered importing ice from Norway. Seeking reassurance their orders would be filled, these merchants crowded the office of Charles B. Church, president of the Independent Ice Company, to pepper him with questions.[6] Church had once been a partner of a Georgetown lumber merchant and knew all about Maine as a source for construction lumber and now for its enormous ability to provide ice as well.

During this interview he said that his company owned nine huge ice-

"An Immense Vessel"

houses on the Kennebec River, each accommodating a minimum of 36,000 tons of ice during a winter, and employing hundreds of men and horses, wagons and specialized equipment to scrape, groove, cut, and haul the ice into the houses. Other Maine rivers produced ice but their waters were impure. The Androscoggin had large cotton factories at Lewiston Falls whose refuse soiled the river. Further north, the Penobscot served lumber mills whose sawdust impregnated the ice. The Kennebec story was different. Rising in the Moosehead Lake region in the northern part of the state, and fed by many mountain streams nearly its entire length, its rapid current prevented the formation of bubbles. Consequently, its ice lasted longer in the warehouse and in the hold of a schooner, and was unsurpassed for purity. The shipbuilding industry of Maine, indigenous and alert, was quick to recognize the potential of this trade, and particularly, the shipyards of Bath where skilled master builders practicing a traditional local skill were available.[7]*

Backed by superior amounts of capital, the coal companies of New England, several based in Taunton, were probably the first to develop the roundtrip concept. Representing an insatiable market for ice, Georgetown and Washington became ports of first priority. Moreover, if a vessel put in at Georgetown to unload, it had only to be towed fifty yards or so to the east to tie up at a coal wharf. Here it could load a full cargo of coal whose market at the northern end was equally insatiable. When this trade got under way, it proved a bonanza for the Georgetown waterfront and its merchants, and indeed for the entire community there, ranging from shippers through stevedores and coal heavers (walking over from Rosslyn

*More than two-thirds of the schooners traced for this research were built in the drydocks of Bath, Maine.

Loading coal at a Georgetown dock, in 1872.

and Arlington for work) to the barkeeps busy all day and most of the night slaking the laborers' unquenchable thirst.

Today it seems incredible, but between 1880 and 1900 and into the next decade, at least two thousand two-, three-, and four-masted schooners were logged as putting in and clearing out of Georgetown harbor, mostly loaded with coal on their outbound voyage, but sometimes with guano, other fertilizers and grains.[8] So many came that it was necessary to abandon wharfage west of Wisconsin Avenue, and move east to build adequate facilities on the Mole. The Mole was the broad, peninsula-like embankment built by the C&O Canal Company to create a pond at the terminus of the canal at the mouth of Rock Creek where canal boats could unload coal and turn around to enter the canal heading west for the return trip. With better facilities, schooners made the roundtrip, New England-Georgetown, three and four times a season.

These schooners were among the most economical and efficient carriers ever designed and built. Averaging a gross tonnage of around one thousand, the two- and three-masters measured about 200 feet long, 35 feet wide and 10 to 15 feet in draft; the four-masters had dimensions similar to those of the *White*. Using no fuel, they required only two men to a mast and could carry tonnage as large as a square-rigger with about one-third the crew.[9] By the early Nineties this commerce had grown so active that the four-master with its larger cargo capacity began to drive out the smaller schooners. It became a common sight to see six and eight tall ships, each flying the house flags of a well-known fleet, queued up at Winship's on the Mole waiting their turn at the loading platform.

Meanwhile the Georgetown waterfront economy was changing. Due to the effects of the ubiquitous, contaminating coal dust and smut, and to the erratic supply of water-power from the canal caused by storm damage to canal walls, floods, and drought, five of the seven flour mills had closed down permanently by 1890. Their failure meant that several hundred coopers, millrights, mechanics, and semi-skilled laborers became unemployed. Some found work in the lumber yards along 31st Street, in the developing commercial warehouses in Foggy Bottom, or at the American Ice Company at the foot of 31st Street, where Charles B. Church had torn down five brick warehouses of the federal period and ensconced his thriving presence in a frame warehouse at the southwest corner connecting with piers set back from the edge of the wharf.[10] G. E. F. Key, librarian at the Martin Luther King Library, grew up on Thomas Jefferson Street opposite the new warehouse. He remembers how the masts reared high above the rooflines, and how his mother would send him over to bring home a twelve-inch cube of ice costing a dime.

The coaling schooners may have brought prosperity but they also brought trouble. Shippers would usually pay off their crew at the coal port and not sign on another until the schooner was loaded and ready for sea.[11] The results of having many hard-bitten, hardy, tough sailors on the loose, who were not abstemious and whose year-round struggle with weather,

"An Immense Vessel"

cold and searing heat, sleet, fog or rain called for strong stimulant and relief, is better left to the imagination. Chances were strong that a man might sail in and out of a port for several years and never wander further than a few blocks from the docks. In Georgetown he need move no further than the M Street strip to find cheap drink. Moreover, the red light district lay just south of it in the rowdy, violent neighborhood of interlocking steep little streets, alleys and courts known as "Boston."

"Boston" had its own nomenclature. Below Grace Street, in the warrens around the old milling structures, was "Hungary Hill" where Oisie Ridgley of "Paradise Flats" fired at Jeannette Sims, and the bullet struck a steel rib in Jeannette's corset, saving her life. Below M Street between west Marketplace and 33rd Street flourished "Frog Island," "Boston's" east boundary, where anyone could buy a shot from Bill Davis, the "walking speakeasy." A block west was "Buzzard's Roost," the former Henry Foxall mansion, now a shabby boardinghouse and flophouse, where a furtive Red Bill of Herring Hill would hide out to elude the coppers.[12]

As time went on, there were more and more foreigners among the crews. By the Nineties no more than one-third of the seamen were American, the rest being predominantly Scandinavian or German. The formation of the Atlantic Coast Seamen's Union, which merged with other groups in 1892 to form the International Seamen's Union, an affiliate of the American Federation of Labor, led to the ship-owners hiring non-union Bravas (Negroes) from the Cape Verde Islands.[13] In the Nineties a summer night's crowd along M Street would equal in numbers, if not in age or background, what police find there today. Brawls among this salty, ethnic mix were common, and the coppers would pack the Black Maria every Saturday night with so many prisoners they could scarcely close the door. "It was more crowded than the poundwagon," the *Star* reporter was told.[14]

But by 1910 the spectacular tall ships were approaching their demise. Georgetown might provide a faster loading schedule than other ports but it had the disadvantage of a site on the curve of the river. Strong currents continually swept down mud and debris, much of which settled along the waterfront. Indeed, the weight of a ship's cargo would sometimes prevent it from mooring at the wharf and force it to anchor in the channel where coal would be brought out on canalboats and hoisted aboard by means of a floating elevator.

Moreover, captains considered Georgetown a dangerous place to winter in. Here the full force of floating ice was always felt, for the wharves lay in the track of the ice sweep. By contrast, Washington wharves were protected by the long, paramecium-shaped island stretching south from the Long Bridge, constructed in the Nineties by the Army Engineers to create a wharfing situation undisturbed by weather problems.

Two other factors contributed to the demise of the four-master. One was the emergence of the more economic tug with its string of loaded barges. The other was the purchase on June 22, 1910, by the Baltimore & Ohio Railroad, of the land adjacent to the Mole on the west. Here it intended to build a railroad terminal.[15]

XV

What's in a Name?

Despite the general optimism of the 1880's, there was a burr under the saddle; Georgetown faced an identity crisis. Would it survive as Georgetown, or would it become known now and forever after as "West Washington - ex-Georgetown" as the *Star* often called it? The D.C. Commissioners had already started using this opprobrious term, and many letters to the *Star* in the early Eighties showed how bitter a pill this was to swallow. For its economy to become melded with that of Washington could be accepted. But to lose its mystique, to have its special folklore and the aura informing its name since colonial days purloined and then sublimated with that of the capital city, would be a crushing humiliation. Without a past distinguished from that of Washington, that parvenu city, how could one respect where one lived? This was, indeed, a worry to try the soul.

The first to detect the threat was John McGill, editor of the *Courier*. Early in January 1872 he reported a "design on foot to obliterate by legislative enactment the name of Georgetown,"[1] His words were an omen of a sequence of blows. In 1874 the House Committee on the District prepared a bill to abolish the Georgetown postoffice and in December 1877 it became a branch of the Washington postoffice.[2] Then the District surveyor was spotted renumbering the squares (blocks) to correspond with those of the capital.[3] Another move converted the colorful and original colonial streetnames like Gay and Frederick and Beall into numbers and letters. In 1880 new address-numbers for the houses were distributed to residents. Some took this seriously and replaced the old digits or painted new ones over the old in the fanlights. Others deliberately confiscated them. One exasperated resident complained: "It looks odd to see adjoining houses, one numbered 3300 and the other 32. Let's have uniformity, one way or the other.[4]

But the stubborn small merchants would not be pushed about. One hot morning in September 1886, a cadre of District workmen came to plant shade trees on Wisconsin Avenue between M and N. Immediately, like so many prairie dogs, the shopowners popped out of their shops, declaring they did not want any shade. If the trees were planted, they would cut them down. The foreman was notified. He ordered the men to refill the holes, replace the bricks, and quit. Which they did. And the merchants retired into their hot little shops, perspiring but satisfied.[5]

Georgetown Life, 1865-1900

How to handle the heading for the daily Georgetown news column confused the *Star*. Vacillating between "West Washington i.e., Georgetown" and vice versa, by 1881 it had settled on "West Washington née Georgetown," where it remained until 1889. Abruptly, however, in November, 1889, the *Star* reversed itself. From then, until it was discontinued altogether in 1908, the column was called "Georgetown Doings," or "Georgetown Affairs," or variations thereof.

What accounts for this reversal? Beginning in 1888 and for several years afterwards, a number of events took place which enhanced Georgetown's status. For example, in 1886 the federal government purchased the Aqueduct from the Alexandria Holding Company, closed it to traffic, and began to repair the historic structure.[6] The thing had been a menace and an obstruction for years. The extortionate tolls had discouraged Northern Virginia farmers and drovers from bringing produce and dairy products across the Potomac to sell in Georgetown. When they did use it, cattle fell through the planking into the canal and had to be hoisted out by derricks before they drowned. One gentleman reported the heavy planks of the water trough to be so rotted he could penetrate them with his penknife. These conditions forced the farmers to avoid Georgetown and use the Long Bridge into Washington instead. But now on April 12, 1888, the District Commissioners planned a Georgetown trade fair to celebrate the reopening of the Bridge as a toll-free span. The town was jubilant.

The weather that day was as beautiful as only an April day can be, clear, sparkling, and with fresh green tipping the trees. All sectional bit-

The Aqueduct Bridge where crowds have gathered to watch the flood waters of the Potomac, swollen by the same deluge that precipitated the Johnstown Flood, May 31, 1889. (Courtesy, Columbia Historical Society)

terness forgotten, Congressmen, the Commissioners, and the Virginia delegation chatted amicably together on the little triangle where a fountain played at the intersection of Pennsylvania Avenue and M Street.

General W. H. F. Lee, head of the Virginia delegation, was the main speaker. He retold the glories of Georgetown's past before and during the formation of the Federal City, and continued to recite and extol its part in providing cannon for the War of 1812 from the Foxall Foundry whose foundations were visible upstream. "The site of that foundry is now a manufactory," he said cheerfully. "It's a flour mill," he was told, sotto voce. "Oh, I thought it was a distillery, but didn't want to say so," countered the general amid general laughter. After standing long in the sun, it was clear where his thinking tilted.

After many patriotic speeches and an exuberant explosion of Japanese fireworks and balloons in the shape of elephants, camels, and other zoological specimens, the parade of tradesmen started. Four hundred wagons with displays and eight hundred caparisoned horses plodded through west residential Georgetown past buildings and houses hung with bunting and flags. Among the fifty-eight trades on display, from the Connecticut Pie Company to Birch's Funeral Establishment, only twelve had operated in Georgetown before the Civil War. "It was the most extensive celebration ever held here," concluded the *Washington Post*, "and the citizens would not have sold their birthright for many a mess of pottage."[7]

On this gala day a tradition of travel through Georgetown from South to North, and vice versa, was reactivated. While in the early Eighties only five or six saloons could be found along the stretch of M Street between Rock Creek and the Bridge, by 1890 nineteen were available. As Georgetown developed more and more into the agricultural supply and building trade center it became by 1900, these bastions of goodwill and recuperation became permanent fixtures of the streetscape.

Other evidence of increased trade and prosperity showed up. Small groceries with Virginia produce and dairy products opened on neighborhood corners. Five carriage manufacturers manifested an increasingly mobile and animated society. Communicants' lists at the churches added new names with Virginia connections. At church parties the opening of the bridge provided conversation for months afterward, while plans were made for outings into the Virginia countryside still unfamiliar to most Georgetowners.

Another development tied the maverick town into the District's suburbanizing orbit. In August 1888 the Georgetown-Tenallytown Railroad was chartered.[8] The area north of Georgetown and of Florida Avenue was called the County and had always been considered outside the city limits. In Washington overhead power lines were prohibited. But on this pioneer electric line running outside the capital city's boundaries, no restrictions were placed. Construction and excavation barriers soon barricaded sidewalks, stores, and the front yards of houses the length of Wisconsin

Georgetown Life, 1865-1900

The Georgetown-Tenallytown Railway car at the intersection of Wisconsin Avenue and M Street. The brick building to the right is the F. L. Moore Agricultural Company. Blocked by the streetcar is the John Orme tavern, built in 1762 and torn down in 1921 by the Farmers & Mechanics Bank to build its present, gold-domed building in 1922. It joined the Riggs Bank in 1928.

Avenue to Tenally Circle. Delighted to have access to the fast-growing suburban regions beyond the Weavers' and Barnes' pastures and Holyrood Cemetery, nobody grumbled.

Two years later the light blue cars were running through to Tenallytown. Starting on the waterfront in front of a K Street boathouse, a car would ride up the severe grade to a point north of the canal where, if a freight car, it would normally load Cumberland coal, then change to a double-track and continue up Wisconsin on the east track to Pole Hill at Calvert Street where the steam powerhouse was located on the southwest corner of the intersection with Wisconsin Avenue. If a freight car was loaded with coal, it then ran around the powerhouse to the rear and poured the coal down a chute into the basement.

In such an innovative operation, incidents were bound to happen. In the summer of 1899 a trailer loaded with five tons of bituminous coal got away at the barn crossover at Calvert and ran down backwards into Georgetown on the northbound track, flying at the rate of over a mile a minute. Warning was phoned ahead to O'Donnell's Drug Store at Wisconsin and O Street. The only opposing vehicle was Car 12, the usual afternoon passenger run hauling supplies to people living along the track. The runaway met this train between Dumbarton and N Street. The resulting collision, causing a loud crash heard several blocks away and an explosion of coal dust covering nearby surfaces six inches deep, made town conversation for months afterwards.[9]

What's in a Name?

Despite occasional collisions and many scared and runaway horses, the success of this pioneer line led to the establishment of transportation by electric trolley in all directions, so that by 1900 Georgetown had become the hub of movement of people, packages, mail, produce, and construction material to and from Virginia, Washington and the northwest parts of the District, and in time further out to Rockville and its environs.

Thus, in 1895, in the biggest streetcar deal south of Philadelphia, the Capital Traction Company was formed, absorbing the old Washington & Georgetown Railroad, started in 1862 by Henry D. Cooke, and other District lines. George T. Dunlop was its first president, and no one better fitted to guide Georgetown into its new central role in the District's economy could have been chosen.

Dunlop's career had a touch of the Horatio Alger about it. Related to one of Georgetown's most distinguished early families, he was born in 1845 at "Hayes," the Dunlop farm in Montgomery County. He must have been a strapping youth for he is listed in the 1865 *City Directory* as "farmer." The war years devastated his part of Maryland. Surmising that the South would need all kinds of agricultural equipment and fertilizers in the Reconstruction period, he decided to try his luck in this wide open field. By 1870 he had established his own firm in some warehouses on the west side of Wisconsin Avenue below M Street with access to the canal.[10] Fertilizers soon became one of his most profitable items. Operating out of his sheds, working the same ten-hour day as his forty-one employees, Dunlop saw his gross sales reach $165,000 by 1880.[11] One can only hope his office at 3200 M Street was insulated against the odors produced by mixing and bagging Peruvian quanape lobos, guano, ammoniated bone, super-phosphate, and acids.[12]

By standards of the times, Dunlop became a wealthy citizen. When still in his late thirties, he built his house at 3102 Q Street and lived there until his death in 1908. Wide verandahs surrounded the house and the yard extended down to 1518 31st Street. Dunlop was so hospitable that, in addition to his own large family, he kept the house full of elderly relatives who had no other place to live.[13]

George Thomas Dunlop, 1845-1908
(Courtesy, Emily Ecker Bradley)

Georgetown Life, 1865-1900

Later, as the Northern Virginia and Maryland economy picked up and rural supply centers developed in those areas, Dunlop moved into Capital Traction and ably guided its fast-spreading influence and network through the District from his offices in the Car Barns, the massive, fortress-like building with the prominent tower on M Street at 36th finished in 1897.

In July 1890 the Washington & Great Falls Railroad incorporated, and in 1896 began providing service northwest along the bluffs of the Potomac River as far as Great Falls, Virginia. By 1894 the Washington, Arlington & Falls Church Railway had begun serving suburban Virginia. Other lines established in Arlington and Fairfax counties came across the Aqueduct Bridge, passed through Georgetown, and went on to terminals in Maryland. In only a few years vistas opened up for trade, jobs and sociability previously unimagined.

Although as late as 1895, an Act of Congress abolished the official name of Georgetown from District maps,[14] this proved a waste of congressional breath and printer's ink. The name had become a ubiquitous sign on streetcars travelling everywhere in the District and beyond. It distinguished a growing university, a law school, and a medical school with a hospital. It was the name of a gas light company, and it was the name of an enduring social group, the Georgetown Assembly.

All these events converting Georgetown into a focal place in the District geography had convinced the *Star* it was useless to carry on with the ambiguous "West Washington." And so the editors abandoned it for the more definitive, historic name solidly embedded in the popular mind and vernacular. Georgetown's right to its own centuries-old name was never again disputed.

XVI

Blacks in Residence

In the 1880s a striking feature of the town's residential pattern was its checkerboard quality. Whites and blacks lived in clusters in close proximity to each other, reflecting the generally harmonious racial atmosphere that had characterized Georgetown for a long time. In 1885 the police reported there were 14,332 residents of the town, of which 9,525 were white and 4,807 were black.

If there was little racial tension, there clearly were great differences in the housing of the two races. In 1879 a health survey of the housing on the 107 squares or blocks that constituted Georgetown found 2,549 dwellings and related buildings, such as stables and outhouses, 1,092 of brick and 1,457 of frame. The inspectors rated each dwelling on a scale running from Excellent through Very Good, Good, Fair, Tolerable, Poor to Bad, and discovered only one block in Georgetown (the square bounded by Dumbarton, 30th, N and 31st Streets) which could be rated Excellent. Two blocks were rated Very Good, 27 were Good, 39 were Fair, and the remaining 38 fell below this level. No residence of a black rated more than Fair, and among the black population frame houses outnumbered those constructed of brick by 3 to 1.

In a 15-block area south of P Street on the east side of Wisconsin Avenue was a largely black community known as Herring Hill. Here 1,601 people lived in 47 brick and 146 frame dwellings. Only ten of these were connected to a sewer and only 21 had water-closets. The overall living ratio was 8.3 persons to a dwelling.[1]

Further south on Olive were many black families from Virginia occupying converted stables who worked in Cox's Tannery, at Palmer's Bottling Depot, or as domestics among white families within easy walking distance. On N Street in the 2700 block there was a sharp contrast between the five brick houses on the north side occupied by Naval Observatory scientists and the six little houses on the south side where 46 blacks lived.[2]

Another row of Negro housing had developed on the north side of Q Street just west of Rock Creek Park and was probably one of the pleasanter living sites in the city. The Creek still provided fresh flowing water, foliage and shade in spring and summer, and proximity to the virgin Kalorama woods full of wildlife. In this tangled, thick woods, dogs flushed deer, coon, and possum, and brought back rabbits and squirrels.

Georgetown Life, 1865-1900

Typical of more prosperous Negro families was the Lee household at 2904-06 M Street. Alfred Lee, a mulatto born free and brought up in Georgetown, was probably a son of Aloysius Lee, a Roman Catholic, whose name appears in the 1830s as owning property which later belonged to Alfred. (Aloysius Lee and other family members are buried at Holyrood Cemetery.) Alfred Lee established a feed business, and when he died in 1868, aged 63, left an estate of $100,000, mostly in real estate throughout the District but including $5,200 in his store's inventory, $1,615 in cash at the Riggs National Bank, and five gold watches and a Masonic pin.[3] Adding harness and tack to the traditional inventory of hay, oats and other grain, his sons, John T. Lee and William H. Lee, carried on the business into the 1900s when the motor car began to replace the horse as the principal means of transportation.

By the 1880s some strong and independent black congregations had emerged. The most numerous was that of Mt. Zion United Methodist Church at 1334 29th Street. On the night of July 12, 1880, fire destroyed the old Mt. Zion Church on Mill Street. With the walls of its new structure on 29th Street already five feet up, the congregation used the insurance money from the old church to continue the building program while worshipping at Good Samaritan Church on 26th north of P. The Rev. Edgar Murphy, a Virginia carpenter, supervised the building crew. Women's groups organized festivals and jubilees. Evangelical services and revivals were held to collect money and increase membership. Although the membership was somewhat transient, a core of oldtimers like Alfred Pope organized the congregation to wainscott the church nave, plaster and fresco the walls, and install windows, furnaces, and a new organ.[4] By 1891 the congregation numbered seven hundred, was free of indebtedness, and owned a large cemetery. The *Star* called it "one of the most prosperous churches in Washington."[5]

Well-knit church organizations were not the only catalysts binding the large and scattered black community together. Lodges appeared as early as 1873,[6] along with a myriad of other clubs, circles, secret societies and orders. The Grand United Order of Odd Fellows, or the G.U.O.O.F., may have been the largest and met the most frequently; but the 1890s also produced the Georgetown Patriarchs, a Commandery of the Knights of St. John, the Columbia Lodge, the Potomac Union Lodge, and for younger men, the Progressive League. Most voters were Republican and every political election evoked high and vociferous enthusiasm. More than three hundred attended the McKinley-Hobart rallies in 1895.[7]

The ladies were equally active, and apparently not nearly as self-conscious about it as their white counterparts. The Embury Chapter of the Epworth League, with senior and junior chapters, would celebrate an Old People's Day every year. The Sisters of Mary and the Mite Missionary Society organized lawn parties to raise money for a Home for the Infirm and Aged, and the Ancient Daughters of Tabitha, the Minerva House of Ruth, and the Widows' Lodge all formed about the same time. Men and women led by the Fergusons—John Ferguson was a barber popular with everybody—met in the Hawthorne Social Club and the Heliotrope Circle to hear readings of papers and books by black authors, with each meeting followed by a sumptuous repast, a cakewalk, dancing and singing. A highlight was the Mt. Zion choir enacting "The Pirates of Penzance."

The black community used several sites for their gatherings. The G.U.O.O.F. and other lodges met in a hall at 1403 28th Street and in a second, completed about 1900, at 2732 Dumbarton Avenue.[8] For lawn parties two large vacant lots were used, one at the northwest corner of P and 26th Streets, and the other at the southwest corner of Valley (32nd today) and Q Streets. Owned by Dr. A. B. Shekell, a white physician, this lot stood in a predominantly white neighborhood, and the Ebenezer A. M. E. Church ladies who used it courteously secured local consent before making their arrangements. Still another site was Jacob's Park, known today as Rose Park, east of 27th Street, where baptisms in Rock Creek took place in earlier years.

Outings to the Cycle Clubhouse, just outside the District line on Conduit Road (MacArthur Boulevard), were popular.[9] Sunday picnickers piled into carriages and drove to Chevy Chase Circle for special occasions. Thirty-two blacks from Georgetown had participated in the Spanish-American War. "Colored heroes" of the 9th and 10th U. S. Cavalry were feted at camp meetings, picnics, and receptions during the summer of 1899.[10]

Gradually, however, the size of the black population began to shrink. In 1898 Western High School moved from temporary quarters in the Curtis School on O Street to a handsome, spacious building at the corner of Reservoir Road and 35th Street. Simultaneously, rowhousing for whites was built in the vicinity on meadows owned by the Leonard Mackall family for decades, and white families began moving in to be near the school. For a generation a black shantytown called "Brinetown" had thrived on these open spaces. But now this disintegrated. Whites increased in the area and blacks left, moving east either into Herring Hill or on to Foggy Bottom or southwest Washington, in a long-established migration pattern.[11]

Further south, the construction of Georgetown University and its hospital, plus the disruptions caused by building the massive streetcar terminal of the Capital Traction Company, displaced many families who had moved into the region after the BPW made east Georgetown uninhabitable.

Changing land use south of M Street brought in new Irish labor to work in ice-manufacturing plants and the lumber warehouses as well as blacks moving onto the waterfront from further north. A turbulent scene grew more so when a ravenous pack of mongrel curs invaded the place every day, scrapping over empty dinner baskets thrown out by factory employees. All through this hilly and congested mosaic of steep grades and rocky topography, small alleys and courts developed between the papermill, the soap manufacturing plant, the ice warehouses, the power plants, junkyards and coal yards. It spawned disorderly houses so fre-

Georgetown Life, 1865-1900

quented that police out of uniform and in rough-house clothes would haul off wagonloads of prostitutes and gamblers every Saturday night.

The area had its own nomenclature, Hungary Hill, Paradise Flats and Frog Island together making up the overall region in southwest Georgetown known as "Boston." Here unfolded, night after night, a scene reminiscent of "West Side Story," with colored hoodlums loitering in the alleys to fight gangs swaggering over from Rosslyn. Red Bill hung out here with his gang in the deteriorating shell of the old Henry Foxall mansion on 34st Street below the Canal, then called "Buzzard's Roost." It was a lively, constantly nefarious region.[12]

There was one location, though, which blacks seldom deserted or were forced out of. This was the market space intersection with M Street where a rowdy atmosphere spiked with blarney and southern lingo flourished. Here were three saloons run by the convivial men of Erin, two livery stables, one owned by R. H. Darne from Virginia who always had a highbred stallion to show off, and a barbershop. Horse talk, deals in the marketplace or in the saloon when a stallion was at stud, fast talk in the barbershops, a mingling of smells emanating from stable and bierstube, rendered this place a colorful experience all week long. Roughly one hundred blacks lived in unnumbered dwellings along Potomac Street south of M, part of a steady population there which provided labor for these marketplace activities.

"Buzzard's Roost," the hangout of Red Bill of Herring Hill and his gang in the 1890s, was the old Henry Foxall residence, built about 1800 on 34th Street below the Canal. (Courtesy, Columbia Historical Society)

Blacks in Residence

In 1896 segregation was legalized when the Supreme Court ruled in the famous Plessy v. Ferguson case that separate but equal accommodations met the requirements of the Fourteenth Amendment. Many social historians have considered this late nineteenth century period a devastating time for blacks.[13] Yet in Georgetown at least a healthy atmosphere continued to prevail. The *Star* carried on its extensive coverage of local events in the black community: funerals of oldest inhabitants and former slaves, with identification of former owners; obituaries of popular letter-carriers and barbers; accidents, lurid crime, fresh cases of smallpox, indignation meetings, weddings, evictions that wrung your heart when the Georgetown Hospital construction began, fires and floods and their victims. All received the same full attention from the press, and were written with verve and relish equal to that given to the numerous events involving whites. Except for the first painful years immediately after the Civil War, when the community had to adjust to emancipation, complaints about black activities were never reported in the press.

Although Georgetown's black community consisted largely of poor families, led by a small middle-class elite, they were self-respecting and energetic citizens doing the best they could under often adverse circumstances.

XVII

After-hours in Georgetown in the 1890s
Part One

Even though it was merging economically with the capital city, Georgetown possessed one social advantage Washington would never enjoy. This was an aura of permanence and continuity implicit in the presence of many long-resident families and the institutions which they or their ancestors had founded and which they wanted to preserve. In 1900 there were some five hundred families, black as well as white, who had lived there since the Civil War, half of them established in the antebellum period, some as early as 1800. Their relationships, whether religious, cultural, educational, or commercial, were focused on the Georgetown community.

The town's most visible and enduring social group—and also its most exclusive—was the Georgetown Assembly. Organized around 1810, it drew its members from old Maryland and Virginia families who formed the backbone of antebellum society. Until 1861 the Assembly met in the Pompeian Room of the old Union Hotel.[1] During the war no meetings were held. But Georgetown had always been a dancing town. So in the Seventies the newspapers were again referring to "dress balls" held in the Seminary Hotel ballroom (the Seminary Hotel is now the Colonial Apartments) and, in the early eighties, on the third floor of Forrest Hall (1264 Wisconsin Avenue).[2] This building had acquired an unsavory and chequered history when it became a wartime prison for deserters and the Provost Marshal's headquarters. Afterwards, Bladen Forrest had whitewashed and refurnished it, outfitting a large upper room for fraternal lodge meetings and those of the WCTU. This incompatible milieu was where the Assembly met until a welcome event occurred in 1887.

In October of that year the construction of the Linthicum Institute, a school for boys with a large auditorium on the second floor, was completed.[3] Its location was two doors west of Christ Episcopal Church on O Street. With its predominantly southern-oriented congregation, this church was the spiritual home of the Assembly's leaders and was where their children were baptized and confirmed and attended Sunday School. So the sighs of relief and joy from the board members at finding a setting suitable for presenting their daughters to society and conducting their decorous hops can well be imagined. In addition, the floor turned out to be "the best floor for dancing found anywhere in town."[4] A dais was built along one side for the older generation, wearing gloves and formal attire, to sit and receive each young couple before they began to dance.[5]

A description in the *Star* preceding the long guest list for the first Christmas hop, December 22, 1888, reveals how Washington regarded this group.

> Washingtonians are apt to forget in the hurry of official society that makes the capital so gay during the winter that this town was of little importance, save for its big domed capitol, while the city west of us was a "handsome city noted for the literary advantages and polite society," as the geographies say. There is still a distinctively local society element in Georgetown that has not allowed itself to be absorbed by the growth of the other city in the District of Columbia. This winter they have two dancing clubs that are to our western neighbor what the F.C.D.C. and the Delmonico, the Patriarch and Matriarch balls are to the Ward McAllister 400 in New York City. And pretty Linthicum Hall is their Delmonico. They are the Assembly Club and the Ladies' German Club of Georgetown. The music is good, the supper excellent, and a number of debutantes make their debut.[6]

Georgetown's social stage was modest compared to the picturesque and gorgeous settings of New York City or Bar Harbor society. But it was just as decorous and its participants equally distinguished in their own way, if not as affluent or financially prominent in the nation. Young ladies could be sure of meeting young men not only from the capital city but from throughout the country. The stag line for the Saint Valentine's Day hop of 1889, for example, included civil engineers from New York and Pennsylvania, scientists from the Smithsonian Institution, U.S. Navy officers, Treasury clerks of the middle and higher orders, and young relatives of Assembly members from southern states living in Georgetown while studying medicine or law at Georgetown University. For every belle there was a beau, an ideal ratio.

In the early 1890s these habitués of the dance floor led a fast pace. They not only attended Assemblies, which included the alluring round dances—polka, schottische, and waltz—and even an occasional minuet so that the old could dance with the young. But they also branched out into what had recently become the vogue, the Bachellor's German, an elaborate cotillion in which first the men, then the ladies, chose partners for the next dance, offering a choice of favors.[7] In January 1890, for instance, the same forty-five or fifty couples met four times in one week, on two occasions dancing the German, once at Linthicum Hall and once at the home of the Philip Darneilles at 1627 31st Street, who had a debutante daughter.[8]

The popular German involved many interlocking figures, and, as a *Star* reporter who attended a Washington German said, frequently "lasted as long as a session of the United States Senate."[9] These circumstances converted the dance into an ordeal for certain attendants. One was the poor chaperone, whom the young folk at a German considered particularly useless. At least she could eat a good supper of creamed oysters when the dancers finally stopped dancing in the wee hours. Another was John Coachman, who had to wait outside for his employer's inexhausible daughter in the rain or cold. Still another victim suffered on the floor itself. This was the awkward young man whom the leader, one of whose prime requisites was to be firm, would order about like a private in a military academy.

A competent leader was hard to find. He not only had to know all the steps and changes of this "most fascinating dance in social use," but be able to spot a man usurping the lead and pass him over when his turn came.[10] If some artful dodger stole the favors, he had to call the police. Since everyone wanted a chance to "lead out," he might have to ignore his friends or relations so that the awkward stag or the wallflower could receive his special attention.[11] Obviously a neophyte Assembly member would not suit.

In most cases the leader was a man. But in Georgetown this indispensable person was Miss Emily Beall. Her first appearance as leader showed she had much to learn. In 1888 forty-five couples met at Linthicum Hall to celebrate Leap Year with a German. "Miss Emily Beall who led the German well nigh excited the animosity of the men, if she were capable of exciting so unpleasant a feeling, by the force with which she executed the arduous duties. Miss Rittenhouse, on the other hand, received a large portion of good feeling and devotion for the effective management she has given in the most quiet way to these events."[12] In 1889 and 1890, however, Miss Beall still was the leader. So we may conclude that she had achieved more tact and grace in fulfilling this demanding role, and that Miss Rittenhouse was no longer available.

The Assembly's directors constituted a singularly homogeneous group of people. With the exception of William Laird, Jr., who lived at 3337 N Street in Cox Row, all fourteen resided east of Wisconsin Avenue. Ten had been born and had grown up in Georgetown well before the Civil War to parents born themselves either in Georgetown or on a southern Maryland plantation. Philip A. Darneille, a native of Virginia who had married a fourth-generation Georgetowner, was an exception. During the Civil War most were southern sympathizers. Dr. John S. Billings, who had been head surgeon at the Union officers' hospital in Miss English's former seminary, was unusual in this regard. Another acceptable parvenu was Pitt Cooke, Henry D. Cooke's second son, who was divorced. The men were mostly lawyers and bankers who worked in Washington. All owned their homes free of mortgage, having either inherited them or built them themselves.[13]

After-hours in Georgetown—Part One

These people regarded their town as a social and residential community, not one where a living was to be earned. Only one of them had ever been a member of a fraternal lodge or joined with the local business leaders in an association to promote local trade. This was J. Holdsworth Gordon, who with his older brother, William A. Gordon, conducted a law firm in Washington.[14] Both had grown up in Georgetown, and lived across the street from each other, William at 3021 Q Street in Cooke Row and J. Holdworth at 3028 Q Street, a large brick house he had built in 1887. The latter had been a Past Grand Master of the Potomac Lodge No. 5, the District's oldest and most historic brotherhood of Masons.[15]

In the Gay Nineties, the Assembly's belles and their beaux, many of whom came over from Washington, treated the town as if they owned it. And in a sense they did. After all, the setting for their play was the First and Second Additions to Georgetown made by Thomas Beall of George in 1783 and 1785. This was where their direct ancestors had bought property and built houses and where they themselves lived or had grown up. Spring and fall they held hare and hound paperchases that started at 31st and P Streets. Racing east on P to 30th, the hares tore through Cooke Park (an undeveloped brambles until 1894), out Lovers Lane, across Rock Creek, which they had to swim, and after one and a half panting and perspiring hours back to the starting point. Half an hour after the hares set forth, the hounds began their pursuit, with the winner receiving a handsome lover's-knot scarf pin as a prize. Or the hares might head out Reservoir Road and Canal Road, across Chain Bridge, south along the Virginia shore, and back over the Aqueduct Bridge. "Very strenuous," commented the *Star* reporter who was apparently a hound, "but worth a gold award."[16]

A civic sense motivated other agreeable events, such as the fruit and flower festivals staged by the ladies for their churches. Two suitable mansions, unoccupied and spacious, were available: the Cooke mansion at 1517 31st Street, still unsold after the bankruptcy of Jay Cooke in 1873 and used occasionally for bazaars by St. John's Church; and that of Joseph Libbey, the former lumber merchant who died in 1866, at 3043 P Street. In the Libbey garden, one May day in 1896, thirty fond mothers placed their children, aged three or younger, on exhibition, charging admission and giving the proceeds to Children's Hospital.

Unaccountably, in the fall of 1897 the Assembly disbanded. When the secretary sent out the usual cards in the summer, she had only meager response.[17] However, this did not mean that this active, close-knit group dispersed. Presently, in November 1898, the same leaders, acting as members of St. Mary's Guild, Ladies of Virginia, organized a 'bal poudre,'' a charity ball to raise funds for Children's Hospital.[18] Ten years earlier they had also organized the Tudor Place Lawn Tennis Club, with both men and women members, and were so proud of their club that when the *Star* published an inaccurate membership list, they had the list reprinted correctly two days later.[19]

Then, on February 9, 1900, two hundred people, former members

Georgetown Life, 1865-1900

of the Assembly, gathered at Linthicum Hall to plan a new club, the Dumbarton Club. Conceived along the lines of a country club, the membership was to be limited to 300 and the clubhouse to be at the residence known as Mount Hope on R Street near Wisconsin Avenue. Tennis courts, croquet grounds, bowling alleys and golf links were to be established.

The leadership was nearly identical with the Assembly leadership: J. Holdsworth Gordon, president; Mrs. Emily C. Matthews, first vice-president; David Rittenhouse, second vice-president; and Walter Wheatley, third vice-president. Gordon was in his fifty-fourth year and Mrs. Matthews, whose husband Charles, had died six years before, in her sixty-third. Most had children who would enjoy this kind of a meeting-place and its myriad chances for athletic activity.

On Decoration Day weekend a vaudeville entertainment was planned to celebrate the club's opening.[20] In the Nineties, following a practice unacceptable or not even thought of today, an evening's program might well be built around takeoffs of black vernacular custom, dialect, and minstrelry. Guests or performers would dress up in sporty-looking clothes, black their faces with burnt cork, and paint absurd red lips in a wide grin as part of the act. So on vaudeville night at the Dumbarton Club, the crowd was not disappointed. They were treated to the fashionable black-face entertainment. (How Georgetown's blacks reacted to this parody is not recorded. But in New York's Harlem blacks scorned the whites' poor imitations of their customs and songs.)

Everyone's favorite number was held for the last. This was a cakewalk, than which nothing was more popular with every class of society, black or white, whether the sponsoring group was the Heber Tent of Rechabites, Georgetown's oldest temperance organization, the Young People's Society for Christian Endeavor, or the Dumbarton Club.[21] All were infatuated with the ebullient strut which had originated with Negroes in the south, especially Florida, and was performed by former slaves on the big plantations.[22] Head thrown back, arms folded cross the chest, and body arched backwards, the dancer would walk balancing a container of water on his head, with a prize of a decorated cake awarded to the one who did not spill any. When the dance reached New York, special clubs were formed and competitions held, the best men performers receiving a champion belt, and the women a diamond ring.[23] In the Nineties few entertainments were successful without the cakewalk.

But dancing was not only a recreation of the Georgetown elite. With the singles population in the District increasing steadily, Henry Schlosser (born in Georgetown in 1864) decided that his future need not be as a confectionary salesman or a shoemaker like his German immigrant father. He would be a dancing teacher. Calling himself Professor, in 1895 he opened his first academy on the second floor of a building at the northwest corner of 31st and M Street, which had a public hall.[24] Here he ran what today would be called mixers. Having learned the round dances from his parents, he doubtless taught these lively steps, but since a German required

After-hours in Georgetown—Part One

a chair for each person and thus a minimum of fifty or more chairs, as well as favors, he finessed this expensive dance for financial reasons. His emphasis was on sociability, pure and simple, as a legitimate end in itself.

Following this philosophy, he gave Hallowe'en dances, outdoor and Easter soirées, ribbon dances, pound parties to which every guest brought an edible package weighing a pound, and Leap Year dances. During the spring and summer season of 1896, when the Washington and Great Falls Electric Railroad began to operate, he took all his guests out to the hotel at Cabin John.[25] On June 30, 1896, the Metropolitan Electric Railroad, which had been running between the Connecticut Avenue region and Georgetown for over twenty years, extended its line to Capitol Hill and Lincoln Park.[26] This brought people living in those residential areas to within easy riding distance of Georgetown. A fast operator, Schlosser found that 3007 M Street, a big three-story brick house with a large second-floor hall, needed a tenant. Moreover, its entrance was only a few steps from the trolley stop. He moved in immediately, and sent out cards for an opening fall hop at his new address.[27]

In addition to Schlosser's, four more dancing academies were flourishing in Georgetown in the Nineties. All were organized by Washington residents who rented Schlosser's former, less glamorous quarters, or the Masonic Hall over Weaver's Hardware Store which could hold 350 guests, or sometimes Linthicum Hall. The guest list of these five academies grew in direct ratio to the Washington population. The mise-

Charles Dana Gibson's Girl and her beau in the country. 1900

Georgetown Life, 1865-1900

en-scene chosen by all was Georgetown. Even then, it was becoming known as "Fun City."

Whereas the surnames of the Assembly guests listed in the *Star* were widely known because they came from old local families, those attending the Professor's classes and those of his colleagues were almost totally unfamiliar.[28] City directories of the period reveal that the pupils represented a bourgeois mix—dressmakers, typists, telephone and wireless operators (these were men or women), bakers, conductors, teachers, men in the building trade, and government and merchandizing clerks. They lived along the trolley route, and many came from the West End where George Washington University sprawls now. As many as thirty or forty unmarried women might be listed in a newspaper story without any mention of married chaperones. What were all these young women doing, running around town unchaperoned at night?

They were part of a new breed. This decade may have been called the Gay Nineties, but it was also known as the Gibson Girl Era. Therein lay startling implications. In the Eighties, Charles Dana Gibson, a young Boston artist, had begun to publish in *Life*, a humorous weekly magazine, and later in *Scribner's Magazine*, pen and ink drawings gently satirizing affluent society. The girls stood tall and statuesque, had wasp waists, voluptuous bosoms, and luxuriant hair, piled high in a pompadour under a picture hat or pulled back and tied in a Psyche knot. During the day they

Bicycling near Georgetown (Courtesy, Columbia Historical Society)

After-hours in Georgetown—Part One

wore the Gibson Girl trademark, the tailored shirtwaist; by night, off-the-shoulder decolletage accentuated by leg-o'-mutton sleeves.

In Gibson's sketches, these vibrant, determined young women could be seen pedalling knee to knee with their male counterparts, in and out between horse carriages and hacks, leaving many a placid nag wild-eyed with fright. And indeed Georgetowners saw the Gibson Girl en masse. In the summer of 1898 a larger number of bicycles passed through Georgetown than any other precinct in the District.[29] As Fairfax Downey said in his "Portrait of an Era," the Gibson Girl sped along joyously, women's rights perched on her handlebars and cramping Victorian attitudes—including the need for a chaperone—strewn in her wake.[30]

With her image, reproduced by the millions in Gibson's telling illustrations, she soon mushroomed into a national cult. There were Gibson Girl corsets, hats, china, and wallpapers. Schlosser's pupils, and those of the Bon Ton Academy and the others, were Gibson Girls in their imaginations, as they cavorted about in a bevy on the trolley. Though probably country-bred and sending money home, they tasted social freedom for the first time and loved it.

XVIII

After-hours in Georgetown in the 1890s
Part Two

If Georgetown had become popular with people who liked dancing, it had also turned into a Mecca for all kinds of other recreational activity. The tempo and scope of public life were accelerating and broadening. Men looked for escape from the confinement of office work. Encouraged by women's new attitudes, they responded with an equally exuberant urge to socialize. In addition to the parish halls of several churches, Georgetown offered a round dozen or more convenient and attractive other halls to choose from for meetings and assemblies, depending on the size or nature of the club or occasion. Clubs of all kinds, social, literary, athletic, cultural, sightseeing, and musical, proliferated. The "No Name," the Nameless"

This photograph was given the author by Cuthbert R. Train in 1977 when he was with Fitch, Fox and Brown, Realtors. "This is a picture of my father (Admiral Charles Russell Train, once of Georgetown) and pals; he is at far left in the front row and this is their baseball squad which operated as a private team in the early '90s. At a younger age when these fellows weren't playing baseball, they belonged to a group called the Kat Killers Club. As a baseball team they were called the Jeffersons. In those days everyone had large side or back lots, and they played other teams on their own grounds."

After-hours in Georgetown—Part Two

(different group), the "Old Bachellors," and the "Oberons" each in turn rented the Potomac Boat Club's airy hall on the riverbank at the foot of 31st Street for a dance. They held euchre parties at Stohlmann's Ice Cream parlor while gobbling up cakes and confections dolloped with whipped cream. They had baseball clubs. The Altair Cycle Club and the "Don't Worry Circle" not only danced at the Boat Club but arranged all-day excursions and picnics around the Dalecarlia Reservoir. Renting the spacious Masonic Hall, the Cycle Club staged a Parcheesi tournament during the February doldrums, which lasted a month, and again at Stohlmann's another time. Ten young gentlemen organized the C.I.B. (initials unidentified) club to develop the physical and mental powers of its members. Any novelty was an excuse for a party. In June 1896, for instance, a printer and publisher gave an "Incubator Party" at his house where "guests were treated to the sight of seeing young chicks appear by artificial means."[1] Spectator sports were popular now. Police from four precincts were called to handle crowds at Georgetown University when its football team played that of the University of Virginia.

The search for outlets away from home and office took thousands onto the river from June through September, when the excursion season was at its height. Some took the refitted antebellum steamer *Mary Washington* to Glymont, a pleasure resort thirty miles down the Potomac on the Maryland side.[2] The steamer *Bartholdi* was also available for charter. So many excursionists preferred the night, when it was cooler, that the harbormaster begged the Commissioners for a night force of police.

> At night time [he reported] the harbor is frequented by disorderly persons in small boats, by nude bathers who offend passersby and apparently give free rein to their lawless propensities, knowing that the harbor police boat is tied up at 7 p.m. and that they are likely not to be molested.[3]

Analostan Island, reached by ferry or boat, was another popular destination. Here the Rod and Gun Club and the Hot Foot Club met, and baseball games between neighborhood teams were played. Then, over the causeway into Virginia, lurked the tantalizing gambling dens of Rosslyn. Beyond Rosslyn, another lure was a gypsies' camp from which young bucks reported in a whisper that they planned to "abduct" some girls. Needless to say, these diverting forays were stag affairs and strictly on the q t.

The same outreach prompted many and varied efforts toward cultural improvement. In 1877 Henry D. Cooke and a few others had organized a Georgetown Amateur Orchestra. After a few years enthusiasm dwindled and the members dispersed. But when interurban transportation improved and many musical Germans wanted a part in the community's cultural efforts, it revived and gave concerts. In 1900 an orchestra of over eighty persons, almost two thirds of whom played the violin and other stringed instruments, drawn from all over the District, presented an ambitious pro-

Georgetown Life, 1865-1900

gram at the Lafayette Square Opera House, playing the overture to "Der Freischutz," Schubert's "Unfinished Symphony," the Grieg concerto for piano and orchestra, and a violin solo by Saint Saens performed in unison by 40 violins.[4] At the same time Mozart and Mendelssohn Clubs were formed. Musicales were given in honor of visiting guests. Church groups presented "The Mikado" and "The Pirates of Penzance." Mandolin and guitar duets, and vocal and whistling solos, were popular as "expressions of spring" in the parlors and Sunday School halls of Georgetown churches.

Although public appreciation of instrumental playing was well developed by the Nineties, that for art as a form of leisure-time pleasure was relatively late in evolving. But if Washington had its William W. Corcoran, Georgetown had Thomas E. Waggaman, a wealthy real estate broker. An affable man with a long and distinguished colonial Maryland background,[5] he lived at 3300 O Street with his wife Charlotte from Louisiana and their five children, well cared for by five servants. On the west side of his house, where there were north-facing windows, he had built an art gallery forty by eighty feet in size. Begun as a hobby in the early Eighties, Waggaman's buying and hanging of his many canvases became an absorbing pastime.

The collection could not boast such a drawing card as Corcoran's "Greek Slave," but it did include works of the Barbizon School and watercolors and oils by the Dutch masters.[6] The Waggamans were Roman Catholics, and consequently many visiting groups came from parochial schools in the District, as well as from convents and monasteries. Meetings and talks to explain artistic techniques were held to benefit Catholic church charities. In the evolution of Washington's place today as an artistic center of the first water, the Waggaman gallery was a benchmark along the way.

Diverted as the public was by art and music, this interest could not hold a candle to its fascination with current events, national and international. In earlier decades, obsessed as it was to preserve its independence from the federal city, Georgetown had led an almost sheltered, insular life. Now this became impossible. In 1898 the Spanish War built to a climax, and many young Georgetowners followed Teddy Roosevelt's Pied Piper figure down to Florida and then Cuba. Residents traveled far from home, making sentimental journeys back to the Old Country to see where they had been born or to visit a son studying violin in Munich. Groups formed to visit the wild Klondike region in Alaska. In 1896, two residents attended the coronation of the last Russian czar, Nicholas II, one returning to America via Venice and the other via Persia. Back in Georgetown, they were eager to describe their strange and wonderful experiences.

With more efficient stoves, the wide use of ice to preserve food, the invention of the washing machine (as well as the useful presence of nine Chinese laundries in Georgetown), and the expanding role of the telephone, entertainment at home became easier. Parties were given with travel talks and stereopticon slides, such as a report on a journey to visit a wounded sailor in a Manila hospital after the Battle of the Philippines in the spring

After-hours in Georgetown—Part Two

of 1898. Missionaries to Japan gave accounts of their experiences. Young men's groups debated whether the United States should retain the Philippines or give the islands their independence. The affirmative side in favor of retention enjoyed an overwhelming victory, and the debate prompted people to hack over to Fort Myer to hear the Sixth Cavalry's band giving the colors a patriotic salute.

Escalation in lodge activity was another amalgamating result of improved interurban transporation and an additional proof of Georgetown's enduring attraction. Most men in the trades, whether clerks or proprietors, still worked ten hours a day, six days a week.[7] Yet two hundred people, all Georgetowners, were a common number attending meetings at some of the larger orders and commanderies, such as the Independent Order of Odd Fellows and the Knights Templar of the Potomac Commandery No. 3.[8]

After the Civil War, Washington had seen phenomenal growth in Masonry, so large its own existing halls could not service the many circles, societies, orders, tents, chapters, and commanderies that mushroomed with the growing population. Masonry in what became the District of Columbia had been established in a lodge in Georgetown long before the town was laid out or perhaps even named. The lodge, called St. Andrews, worked under a charter granted by the Grand Lodge of Scotland in 1727. A direct descendant of this lodge in the 1890s was Potomac Lodge No. 5, the largest Masonic lodge in Georgetown and certainly the most historic in the District, with headquarters over Weaver's Hardware Store.[9] (You can see carved on the pediment of the store the national Masonic emblem, i.e., the square and compass framing a large G for deity or God.)

Participation in lodge activities was probably the most popular leisure-time pleasure in turn-of-the-century Georgetown. Streets that were tranquil by day, like Olive and Dumbarton or the northern reaches of 34th and 35th Streets, were animated by night with printers, tilesetters, jewelers, mechanics, motormen, and the like trudging in all weathers to their lodge meetings.

Though each lodge had a different schedule, they all followed a certain routine. There was the annual inspection of books and paraphernalia by grand masters, past grand masters, the venerable master, or the noble grand master, each official in full-dress uniform. Another formal occasion was the installation of officers. Still another was the donning of full-dress uniform to visit a sister lodge in Washington. At these times the members did not march. They took the trolley, monopolizing the entire vehicle.

Providing Threlkeld School at 36th and Prospect with a flag was a typical lodge enterprise. The school, the oldest in town, had neither a flag nor a pole to fly it on. A week after the planning session, the members of the United American Mechanics gathered at 3 p.m. at their hall at 31st and M Streets to join with Company H of the Western High School cadets and parade over to the school. The band of the National Guard led the formation, marching from M and 31st to 29th, then up to N, over to

Georgetown Life, 1865-1900

Wisconsin, up to Q, over to 35th, then south again to O, over to 36th, and finally up to the school. With a blaring of trumpets the flag was raised and saluted on a pole installed by the mechanics.[10] Such ceremonies were frequent. New "tents" often merged with others. When IOOF Covenant Lodge No. 13 combined with Mechanics No. 18, the former became the "banner lodge in the District with over 200 members." A year later 112 new members had been initiated[11]

Sociability was important too. Wives or "lady friends" accompanied their husbands or friends at an annual program that would be musical or dramatic, or in August, gastronomic. These events featured ballads, blackface monologue, oyster roasts and watermelon feasts, waxworks, and skits prepared by the ladies, with such titles as "How He Popped The Question" or "The Long-Lost Nephew."

This participation brought women off their front porches and out of their parlors and kitchens. They began to form auxiliaries. At first, during the winter of 1897, when they discussed organizing the Mizpah Chapter No. 8 of the Order of the Eastern Star, the expectant members were sworn to secrecy.[12] But finally, on June 29, 1898, the news was out. To celebrate, thirty-five middle-aged matrons, uniformly wives of leading local businessmen, pulled out all the stops. They staged a three-day lunch and supper bazaar with oysters, a cakewalk, and a taffy pull. Although the Treaty of Paris had yet to be signed, the victory over Spain in the Philippines had been won. So it was appropriate to present an elaborate tableau called "Columbia, the Pride of our Boys," representing the American soldier and sailor clasping hands, with Columbia's arms around each and the Spanish flag at her feet. A kind of euphoric patriotism seized the women. A year later the chapter's membership was one-third larger.[13]

Then, as the decade reached the century's turn, there developed an exciting new form of pleasure, the excursion by electric trolley out into the countryside west of town. In 1895 the Capital Traction Company's huge stone terminal was built with a station on Prospect Avenue at 36th Street.[14] Here on August 23, 1894, the Washington and Great Falls Railroad initiated service on its route to Cabin John and Great Falls. Construction of the line had presented engineering challenges, such as elevated trestles and bridges over streams and roadbeds that the interurbans never had to confront. At its start the line provided a reassuring surprise: it passed right through an operating dairy barn with cows on each side, some being milked. Later, it settled down to running high on the bluffs and palisades overlooking the river. Views of heavy woodland would be interrupted by impressive scenes of fast-flowing water and formidable stone quarries on the Virginia side. At times the track paralleled the C&O Canal and passengers looked down in wonder at the loaded barges crawling at the mules' pace on the green-brown water of the canal below.[15]

Near the District line the trolley passed the International Athletic Club's wide race-track. Here most people in this cycling epoch knew about or could imagine the action under the frame grandstand in the training

After-hours in Georgetown—Part Two

quarters. Each trainer had his special ointment or formula, which was regarded as a profound secret with magical powers if properly applied. The muscles of the racers had to be kneaded just so and massaged scientifically as if by a chiropractor. Some riders would be in ten races and each time undergo an equally vigorous rubdown.[16]

After the Athletic Park came the stone amphitheatre at Glen Echo built by the Chautauqua Association and used by religious groups for services and ceremonies accompanied by a grand organ. (The amusement park on this site was not opened until 1910.) At this point a group might get off for a picnic, then catch a later trolley to continue the tour to Great Falls, where the Potomac drops from a seventy foot elevation over majestic rock formations to create boiling and foaming white water. But before the Falls came the magnificent sight of the Cabin John Bridge, also known as the Union Arch, an engineering feat touted around the world as the widest span over a ravine anywhere.

The Civil War was still within the vivid memory of most middle-aged adults. Thus, a special curiosity at the bridge was the plaque laid in the west abutment where the name of Jefferson Davis, Secretary of War when war was declared, had been erased in 1862 by order of Caleb B. Smith, Secretary of the Interior. (It was later restored by President Theodore Roosevelt.) Families with picnics could stop at the Cabin John Hotel run by the Bobbinger brothers, who always had plenty of lemonade or something stronger on hand. Small wonder this ride soon became the best-known suburban route in the District and remained so well into the second half of the next century.[17] It knew no social boundary lines.

The impact of the electric trolley, whether one went to work or play, shop or pray, cannot be overemphasized. Along with electricity, the motor-car, and the telephone, it was one of the turn-of-the-century changes that erased the District's old city boundaries and particularly gave women wings and seven-league boots. The yeasty input of the Nineties prefaced a revolution in lifestyle and social emancipation unequaled since.

A Postscript

These chronicles go no further than 1900 for several reasons. Four years ago when I stopped the research and began to consolidate it, the 1910 census was still closed to the public. (It has since been opened.) Second, the *Evening Star*, from which I drew much of my material, had by 1900 become a large newspaper with ten or more pages, much advertising, and many photographs. Georgetown news grew increasingly hard to find. In addition, because of the town's diminishing social and economic status vis-a-vis Washington, there was less of it.

Third, and perhaps most important, by the turn of the century, Georgetown itself had markedly changed. Essentially it had stopped growing. From 1880 to 1900 the population had increased from 12,578 to 14,549, but the net growth since 1890 had been only 303. The waterfront had become an urban boondocks cluttered by the ugly and polluting buildings and smokestacks of the Potomac Electric Power Company, the gas works, a big rendering plant, artificial ice manufactories, a sheet metal works, and the like. These industries attracted blue collar workers who also liked the low-rental housing being constructed.

Another large group of newcomers were widows who found the low rentals attractive. In 1890 about one hundred women had declared themselves widows to the city directory enumerator. Ten years later, there were five hundred forty; some were longtime residents, but the greater number were new. Clearly, they were not likely to establish a residential tradition. Rather their presence stimulated builders to put up more apartments.

Meanwhile, people were also moving out of the area, drifting toward Foggy Bottom and southwest Washington. Sons of local oldtime families would marry, find housing in the suburbs, and work in Washington. Even executives of local businesses, who had formerly lived in Georgetown, moved into Washington, commuting back to their Georgetown desks by day.

In addition to the major attrition just described, the town wore a depressed look deriving from several circumstances. Big, landmark houses belonging to families who came in the federal era had vanished, and with them a large part of the town's distinctive historic aura as well as open green space. Since newcomers now were not home buyers but tenants, by 1910 virtually all building of single-family homes had stopped. Some one hundred houses were vacant; others of the hitherto most desirable class were now boarding or rooming houses. Cox Row with its five large units sheltered some sixty electricians, telephone or elevator operators, switchmen, and the like. The only privately owned and occupied dwelling in the Row was that of the Forrest family at 3339 N Street. (The family would hold out until 1944 when the last survivor, the 87-year old widow of a Forrest son, sold it to a World War II army colonel working at the Pentagon.) The once-famous Bodisco house, converted now into ten apartments, was another victim of the depression.

In 1900 there were 422 householders listed in the Washington *City Directory* whose families had lived in Georgetown since 1870, and 207 who had lived there since 1860. By contrast, the 1915 *Directory* showed only 121 whose roots went back to 1870 and only 69 going back as far as 1860.

Moreover, pockets of near-slum-like living conditions in the east portion of town, below M Street and around Volta Place, marred any illusions of gentility that might still emanate from the central residential blocks along N, O, Dumbarton, and P Streets. New families coming to Washington who might formerly have selected Georgetown as a place to live, now settled near Dupont Circle or further out in Cleveland Park or Wesley Heights. Despite its proximity to the central city, Georgetown in the first part of the twentieth century had become a somewhat old-fashioned, second-class district, although people living today and growing up in those years say they were unaware of this kind of change.

By 1930 a renaissance was under way. Why and how this dramatic urban development took place has been described in the unpublished Ph.D. dissertation of Dennis Gale, entitled "Restoration in Georgetown, 1915-1965." Written by an astute and scholarly historian, now Associate Professor in the Department of Urban and Regional Planning at George Washington University, it is available at the Peabody Collection in the Georgetown Public Library.

Notes

The following abbreviations are used in these notes:
DNI — *Daily National Intelligencer*
GC — *Georgetown Courier*
LC — Library of Congress
NA — National Archives
RG — Record Group

1 Postbellum Paralysis

1. *Ordinances* of the Corporation of Georgetown, 15 April 1865.
2. *Georgetown Courier*, 29 April 1871. This source, available at the Peabody Room, Georgetown Public Library, was published 1865-1876.
3. Gordon, William A., "Reminiscences of a Boyhood in Georgetown." Unpublished manuscript at the Peabody Room.
4. Boyd, William A., *Washington, Alexandria & Georgetown City Directories*, 1865-1870.
5. *Daily National Intelligencer*, 6 November 1865.
6. Joseph Libbey, lumber merchant, built 1516-1518 31st Street in 1864 for his two daughters when they married.
7. Georgetown Tax Assessment Records, 1865-1869; RG 351, NA.
8. Oberholtzer, E. P., *Jay Cooke, Financier of the Union Army*. Franklin, N.Y., 1907, Vol. I, p. 570. The author regrets she never found this informative, extremely well-documented biography available in the library of the National Archives before her Civil War history of Georgetown, *Divided Town*, was written and published in 1968. The biography contains many letters from Henry D. Cooke to his brother Jay written during wartime, after the Cookes moved into 1517 30th Street in 1862.
9. GC, 8 October 1866.
10. GC, 25 August 1866.
11. Morgan, Maxine Goff, *A Chronological History of the Alexandria Canal*, Part II, Arlington Historical Society, Inc., 1966.
12. GC, 17 July 1867.
13. Obituary, John McGill, *Washington Post*, 19 January 1880.
14. GC, 16 November 1867.
15. GC, 6 July 1866.

Notes

II Drums Along Rock Creek

1. GC, 28 December 1865.
2. Many references could be given for this complex subject. The code worked out differently in Washington than in Georgetown. Two good references used here are Myers, Gus, "Pioneer in the Federal Area," *Records* of the Columbia Historical Society (44-45) page 142, and *History of Washington*, Vol. I, by Constance M. Green (See listing for Black Code and its references.)
3. *Evening Star* May - November 1860, 8, 17 May 1867.
4. *Daily Constitutional Union*, 11 September 1866. This Democratic organ was published in Washington, 1863-1869, and can be read at the Library of Congress.
5. GC, 10 February 1868.
6. *Sunday Morning Chronicle*, 2 March 1862. Published in Washington, 1861-1881. Located at the Library of Congress.
7. Magruder, Dr. Hezekiah, *Cash Books of 1841-1848*, Peabody Room, Georgetown Public Library.
8. Boyd, William A., *Washington, Georgetown and Alexandria City Directories*, 1863-1865.
9. Georgetown Tax Assessments 1845-1865, RG351, NA.
10. *Evening Star*, 20 January 1865.
11. *Ibid.*, 31 March 1866.
12. Green, Constance McLaughlin, *The Secret City*, Princeton, 1967, page 6.
13. *Evening Star*, 7, 13 November 1867.
14. GC, 28 May 1868.
15. *Ibid.*, 28 May 1868.
16. *Ibid.*, 22 February 1873.

III Survival of the Bob-Tail Bull

1. GC, 6 November 1875.
2. *Ibid.*, 19 February 1870.
3. *Ibid.*, 5 March 1870.
4. *Evening Star*, 1 May 1869.
5. GC, 3 July 1869.
6. *Ibid.*, 19 November 1869.
7. *Ibid.*, 4 September 1869.
8. *Ibid.*, 12 September 1870.
9. *Ibid.*, 1 February, 1 May 1868.
10. *Ibid.*, 5 December 1874.
11. News items beginning March 1866, and running frequently through the next five years in the *Georgetown Courier*, showed how long it took to complete this structure and, by the same token, how interested the town was in having it to show off.
12. GC, 5 October 1867.

13. *Ibid.*, 19 May 1866.
14. *Evening Star*, 3 August 1869.
15. *Ibid.*, 29 October, 4 November 1869.
16. *Daily Constitutional Union*, 20 June 1866; GC, 23 June 1866.
17. GC, 17 April 1869.
18. Donovan, bricklayer; Dyer, carpenter; Findlay, bricklayer; Frey, carpenter; Hilleary, bricklayer; Huddleston, slater; Hurdle, bricklayer; Meem, carpenter; Murray, painter; Murtagh, bricklayer; Ogle, painter; Rodier, paperhanger; Sebastian, bricklayer, painter, tinner; Sparshott, plasterer.

IV   Henry D. Cooke—Part One

1. Letter to author from James L. Murphy, reference librarian, 16 July 1979, The Ohio Historical Society, Inc., Columbus, Ohio.
2. Obituary, Henry D. Cooke, *Washington Post*, 25 February 1881.
3. Oak Hill Cemetery Records, Oak Hill, Georgetown.
4. Oberholtzer, E. P., *Jay Cooke—Financier of the Union Army*, Franklin, N.Y. 1907, Vol. I, page 131.
5. *Ibid.*, Vol. I, page 204.
6. *Ibid.*, Vol. I, page 187.
7. See Specific and Ad Valorem Taxes Division, 7 May 1863. Records of the Internal Revenue Service, Department of the Treasury, RG 58, NA.
8. Land Records, D.C., NCT 60, ff 317.
9. *Evening Star*, 29 May 1866.
10. *Ibid.*, 25 October 1890.
11. *Daily Constitutional Union*, 22 September 1866.
12. See will of Laura S.H. Cooke, filed 8 September 1904, Office of Register of Wills, No. 12509.
13. See 1870 census, entry, Henry D. Cooke.
14. Water Registrar's Report to District of Columbia Commissioners, 1875.
15. *Daily Constitutional Union*, 22 September 1866.
16. Land Records, D.C., ECE 10, ff 419.
17. Ordinances of the Corporation of Georgetown, 17 August 1866 and 14 June 1867. If you look today at the elevations of the Episcopal Home, the former Hollingsworth estate on the south side of Q Street, and of Tudor Place on the north, and remember that in that era, one estate ran into the other divided only by a fence, you can appreciate the formidable excavations necessary to create a deep, broad pathway for curbing, guttering and reaching Wisconsin Avenue. Until l869 and generally until 1871-3, when the Board of Public Works was in Georgetown performing plastic surgery on its total face, many hills and depressions marked the entire town. The opening up of Q Street, east of Wisconsin Avenue, for example, invited the idea of opening up Q and R Streets west of Wisconsin Avenue between 34th and 35th Streets. The *Georgetown Courier* on September 30, 1869, said: "This gives a view through to the Academy of the Visitation, one of our most valuable properties, and concealed by the hills which intervened, until now."

Notes

V Henry D. Cooke—Part Two

1. Land Records, D.C., D6, ff 357-377.
2. Beall, William D., *Reminiscences, Washington Post,* 3 July 1932, page 1.
3. Oak Hill Cemetery Records, Henry D. Cooke lot.
4. GC, 13 August 1870.
5. See "Washington Miscellaneous" *Washington City Directory* 1871, page lxxx.
6. GC, 11 June 1869.
7. *Ibid.*, 10 September 1870.
8. *Ibid.*, 11 March 1871.
9. Letter to the author from Josephine Cobb, 12 July 1979, describing the "imperials." Miss Cobb, now retired, is an authority on Matthew Brady. The appointment to photograph the baby is found in the Matthew Brady Appointment Book for June 1870-December 1875, Lot 1146, Division of Prints and Photographs, Library of Congress.
10. GC, 10 June 1871.
11. *Ibid.*, 20 May 1871.
12. *Evening Star*, 4 May 1898.
13. GC, 22 February and 1 March 1873.
14. Oberholtzer, *op. cit.*, Vol. I, page 417.
15. Will of Laura S.H. Cooke No. 12509, RG 21, NA.
16. Obituary, Henry D. Cooke, *Washington Post*, 25 February 1881.
17. GC, 24 April 1875.
18. *Ibid.*, 17 July 1875.
19. *Evening Star*, 1 March 1881.

VI Takeover at Oak Hill—Part One

1. Report of Investigating Committee, DNI, 7 June 1869, page 1.
2. Burial Records, Oak Hill Cemetery.
3. "Oak Hill Cemetery, Its Origin, History, Character, and Condition," DNI, 21 July 1866. This first-class article consumes four full-length columns of the DNI's front page. Its reporter delved into all facts and books available at the cemetery, and persisted against odds until he had the entire story available by June 1866. Many important facts used in this article come from this source.
4. George de la Roche had also been the architect for the U.S. Naval Observatory, 1842-44. He was born in 1790 in Offenbach, Germany, and came to Georgetown to live about 1840. James Renwick, Jr., was also the architect for St. Patrick's Cathedral, New York City, and the Smithsonian Institution building, now called The Castle.
5. U.S. Census, 1870, RG 29, NA.
6. "W.W. Corcoran," unpublished monograph by Mathilde D. Williams, Peabody Room, Georgetown Public Library.

7. *Minutes* of Board meetings, 24 October 1851, Oak Hill Cemetery.
8. DNI, 21 July 1866.
9. *Ibid.*
10. *Ibid.*
11. Cohen, Henry, *The Career Biography of W.W. Corcoran*, Westport, Connecticut, 1971. This book is No. 4 in a series called *Business and Politics from the Age of Jackson to the Civil War*. It is the source for most statements about Corcoran's financial and political career.
12. Renwick-Corcoran correspondence, Renwick Copybooks, Manuscript Division, LC. Reference obtained from James M. Goode, Smithsonian Building.
13. Corcoran to Brown, 25 April and 27 May 1856. Corcoran Papers, LC. (Hereafter Corcoran is abbreviated to "C".)
14. C to Walter, 27 January 1857. C Papers, LC.
15. Summons to C, Circuit Court, District of Columbia, No. 1272, January 1858, RG 21, NA. Also C to Walter, 12 October 1857. C Papers, LC.
16. C to Brown, 27 May 1856. C Papers, LC.
17. Isaac Broome (1835-1922), Associate of the Pennsylvania Academy, 1860, and a Pennsylvania Academician, 1861. Data from Catherine Stover, Archivist, Penn. Academy of Fine Arts, Philadelphia; obituary, *Philadelphia Evening Bulletin*, 5 May 1922.
18. C to Broome, 30 October 1856. C Papers, LC.
19. DNI, 21 July 1866.
20. C to Brown, 23 February 1857. C Papers, LC.
21. Nicholas Acker, *Washington and Georgetown City Directory*, 1858. Stone yard, D north, cor. N. Capitol; obituary, *Evening Star*, 29 October 1877.
22. C to Walter, 12 October 1857. C Papers, LC.
23. C to Brown, 21 July 1856. C Papers, LC.
24. Hyde to Walter, 4 August 1856. C Papers, LC.
25. C to Broome, 4 November, 23 December 1856; 17 July 1857. C Papers, LC.
26. C to Brown, 7 September 1857. C Papers, LC.
27. *Ibid.*, 11 September 1857. C Papers, LC.
28. *Ibid.*, 15 September 1857. C Papers, LC.
29. *Washington News*, 3 October 1857. LC.
30. C to Brown, 2 October 1857. C Papers, LC.
31. C to Broome, 11 November 1857. C Papers, LC.
32. C to Broome, 5 December 1857. C Papers, LC.
33. C to Brown, 7 December 1857. C Papers, LC.
34. *Evening Star*, 17 October 1857.
35. DNI, 21 July 1866.

Notes

VII Takeover at Oak Hill—Part Two

1. DNI, 21 July 1866.
2. Cohen, *op. cit.*, page 207 ff.
3. GC, 13 February 1869.
4. Lotholders' proxies, 19 June 1862, Oak Hill archives.
5. GC, 13 February 1869.
6. Cohen, *op. cit., page 210.*
7. *Minutes*, Board of Managers, 13 March 1863, Oak HIll archives.
8. GC, 6 June 1868.
9. DNI, 21 July 1866.
10. *Ibid.*.
11. *Ibid.*.
12. *Minutes*, 5 September 1867.
13. *Ibid.*, 10 September 1867.
14. U.S. Census 1880, RG 29, NA.
15. *Washington City Directories* 1846, 1853, 1855, 1858; obituary, in *Army and Navy Register* 16 February 1890.
16. *List* edited by Edward W. Callahan, New York. 1969.
17. Scrapbook B, clippings 24 June 1868, Corcoran Gallery Library.
18. Charge 17, C's statement, DNI 7 June 1869. George Altoft, then the District's Georgetown tax assessor, confirmed the exact measurements of the Oak Hill parcels: 12 1/2 acres given by Corcoran 1849; 3 1/4 acres in first Dodge parcel; 4.09 in second Dodge parcel. Total of 19.84 acres in Square 1285, lot 809, and Square 2156, lot 801.
19. GC, 27 June 1868.
20. Charge 18, C's statement, DNI, 7 June 1869.
21. *Ibid.*
22. Charge 7, C's statement, DNI, 7 June 1869.
23. C to J.S. Blundon, 20 October and 23 October 1868. C Papers, LC.
24. Charge 14, C's statement, DNI, 7 June 1869.
25. Charge 19, *Ibid.*
26. Charge 21, *Ibid.*
27. GC, 16 January 1869.
28. Pamphlet mentioned in the GC, 30 January 1869.
29. Card, C to editor, GC, 6 Febrary 1869.
30. DNI, 28 January 1869.
31. Charge 20, C's statement, DNI, 7 June 1869.
32. *Evening Star*, 10 February 1869.
33. GC, 27 March 1868.

34. Proxies, 9 February 1869, Oak Hill Archives.
35. DNI, 15 February 1869.
36. GC, 20 February 1869.
37. Cohen, *op. cit.*, page 360, n 21.
38. Cohen, *op. cit.*, "Renwick, Corcoran, and the Gallery."
39. The Report of the Investigating Committee and C's statement, DNI, 7 June 1869.
40. Deed from James W. Corcoran and others conveying certain lots in Oak HIll to W.W. Corcoran, 14 July 1869. Oak Hill Archives.
41. GC, 12 June 1869.
42. Boyd's *Washington and Georgetown City Directory*, 1868.

VIII "The Impregnable Burg"

1. GC, 21 December 1872.
2. *Ibid.*, 25 May 1872.
3. *Ibid.*, 6 July 1872.
4. *Ibid.*, 31 August 1872.
5. *Ibid.*, 24 August 1872.
6. *Ibid.*, 31 August 1872.
7. Oberholtzer, *op. cit.*, I, pages 357-358.
8. GC, 9, 23 November 1872.
9. *Ibid.*, 31 August 1872.
10. *Ibid.*, 31 August 7, 21, 28 September, 26 October, 7 December 1872, and 26 April 1873.
11. *Ibid.*, 26 April 1873.
12. Fieldbooks, Georgetown Tax Assessments 1871-1874, RG 351, NA.
13. GC, 10 August 1872.
14. Records, Oak Hill Cemetery, 1874.
15. Vouchers, Letters of Administration, Hezekiah Magruder, 7360 OS Records of the District Courts of the United States, RG 21, NA.
16. GC, 26 April 1873.
17. Report of the Auditor of the BPW, Report of the Commissioners of the District of Columbia 1876, page 160 ff.

IX "Georgetown at a Standpoint"

1. GC, 14 December 1872.
2. 1870 census. Dwellings 293-299.
3. *Evening Star*, 17 November 1897.
4. *Ibid.*, 22 March 1887.
5. *Ibid.*, 2 November 1872.

Notes

6. *Ibid.*, 1 August 1874.
7. *Ibid.*, 4 April 1875.
8. *Ibid.*, 3 March 1876.
9. See files in the Peabody Collection marked 3322 O Street and "Bodisco."
10. See Peabody files for 3314 O Street and 3318 O Street.
11. See Peabody file for 3331 O Street.
12. Since colonial days, when Georgetown was first laid out, P Street has been a wide and heavily travelled artery for interesting historical reasons. Until 1809, when the Long Bridge was built to connect Virginia with Washington City, the Virginia statesmen, journeying between Mount Vernon or Monticello and Philadelphia or New York, would habitually cross the Potomac on a ferry running between Mason's (later Analostan, now Roosevelt) Island and the foot of Wisconsin Avenue, then High Street. They then would ride up Wisconsin to P and turn east to cross Rock Creek at the Papermill Bridge, zigzagging down the slope as we do today to reach the Rock Creek Parkway. The route continued out Florida Avenue to Columbia Road and points east and then north. Nineteenth century drovers also used the street to move livestock to Drovers Rest at the intersection of what is now MacArthur Boulevard and Reservoir Road.
13. *Evening Star*, 11 May 1876.
14. *Ibid*.
15. *The Presbyterian Congregation in Georgetown*, 1780-1970. Published by the Session of the Presbyterian Congregation in Georgetown, Washington, D.C., 1971, pages 51-52.
16. GC, 24 April 1869; 4 May 1869.
17. *Evening Star*, 7 December 1877. (Today's postboxes are in the same locations as those listed in the Star 31 December 1877.)
18. *Report* of the Water Registrar, *Report* of the D.C. Commissioners, 15 November 1875, page 309.
19. *Ibid.*, 1886-1887, page 473.
20. *Evening Star*, 11 May 1876.
21. GC, 18 1873, 19 September 1874.
22. See *Constitution and By-Laws* of City Building Association of Georgetown 1883, Ledger 1902-1905, Perpetual American Bank FSB, 1300 Wisconsin Avenue, N.W.
23. GC, 11 July, 12 September 1874.
24. *Report* of the Assessor, *Report* of the D.C. Commissioners 1875, page 225.
25. Assessor's *Fieldbook* 1874-1875, Rg 351, NA.
26. GC, 13 March 1875.
27. *Ibid*. 1875.
28. See pewlist and communicants' Records, St. John's Episcopal Church, 1869-1880.
29. *Evening Star*, 7 and 12 March, 1879.
30. *Ibid.*, 18 March 1879.
31. *Report* of the Auditor, D.C. Commissioners *Report*, 1888-1889, page 75.
32. GC, 18 August 1879.

Georgetown Life, 1865-1900

X The Ludlow Patton

1. Certificate No. NNR68-1807, Doc. 140092. Records of the Bureau of Inspection and Navigation, Certificates on Enrollment or Registry issued at Georgetown, D.C., RG 41, NA.

2. GC, 29 May 1874. This paragraph gives a complete detailed description of the *Patton*'s construction, including the names of the boatyard and foundry in Cumberland, Maryland, which had the contract.

3. *Ibid.*, 29 May 1875.

4. *Ibid.*, 18 March 1876.

5. *Ibid.*, 11 March 1876.

6. Sanderlin, Walter S., *The Great National Project: A History of the Chesapeake & Ohio Canal*. Johns Hopkins University Studies in Historical and Political Science, LXIV, No. 1. (Baltimore, 1946), page 182.

7. Hutchinson, John W. *The Story of the Hutchinsons*, Vols. I, II, Boston, 1896, I pp 105, 108, II pp 230-231.

8. Report of the Secretary of War, 1886, 49th Congress, 1st Sess. 1884, Ex. Doc. 138, No. 3.

9. GC, 30 January 1869.

10. Telephone interview with Sarah Collins, 24 January 1985.

11. Sarah Collins, *op. cit.*

12. Chase, Enoch Aquila, "The Arlington Case," *Records* of the Columbia Historical Society, vol. 31-32, pages 175-207.

XI Newcomers - Male

1. The numbers were determined by checking the 1900 census and Boyd's *Washington City Directory* for names and Georgetown addresses. Only clerks who designated their department were counted.

2. Since the 1890 census was destroyed, to find out the population of Georgetown for that year, the author made her own city directory by listing all Georgetown names, addresses and occupations found in Boyd's *Directory of the District of Columbia*, 1890

3. Garrison, Fielder H., M.D. *John Shaw Billings*, G.P. Putnam's Sons, New York, 1915. Dr. Billings may have been long on ability and experience. But harassed by officials and hospital duties, he was sometimes short of temper. On 20 August 1887, he was charged in Police Court with having assaulted Upton Mackall (probably one of the numerous Mackall clan in Georgetown) by choking him. The defendant said that Mackall said "Awh" and laughed when Billings passed and the latter stopped and put his hand on Mackall's collar saying he had had enough of it. Hopewell Darneille (a Virginia newcomer) testified that the provocation was a grunt and a laugh. The court said it was a trifling case and imposed a fine of $3.00. *Evening Star*, 20 August 1887.

4. Hollerith, Virginia, *Biographical Sketch of Herman Hollerith*. Reprinted from ISIS, Vol. 62, Part 1, No. 210, 1970.

5. 1884-1890   3107 N Street
   1891-1893   3124 Dumbarton Avenue

Notes

      1894-1899   1521 31st Street
      1889-1915   3027 N Street. (This was Dr. Billings's house. By this time he had left Georgetown and was head of the New York Public Library.)
      1917-1929   1617 29th Street. In 1884 Hollerith filed the first of 31 patents on his machines and tabulating system. The last was in 1917. He died in 1929.

6. Hall, Asaph, *Notebooks*, 5 August - 24 September 1877, United States Naval Observatory, Massachusetts Avenue at 34th Street, Washington, D.C. For Dr. Hall's salary see the *Official Register* 1867-1901, Library, National Archives. Salary, place of birth and place from which the officer was appointed are given in this informative listing of all officers, civil, military, and naval in the service of the United States, published in alternate years. Ten other nautical computers, mathematicians and astronomers also lived in Georgetown during this period: Thomas Harrison, Joseph E. Nourse, Mordecai Yarnall, Edgar Frisby (born in England), George B. Whiting, General Henry E. Lockwood, Roberdeau Buchanan, George W. Hill, J. Morrison Cleveland, and Reuel Keith.

7. *History of the Bureau of Engraving and Printing: 100 years 1862-1962*, Treasury Department, Washington, D.C., page 8.

8. Document File–522879, Records of the Adjutant General's Office (94), N.A.

9. Cross, Marion E., *Pioneer Harvests*, The Farmers and Mechanics Savings Bank of Minneapolis, 1949, page 8.

10. Letter in the Tennessee State Library and Archives, Nashville, Tennessee, from Archibald Roane to the Librarian, Mrs. Parmalee Harrell, 12 August 1876. His grandfather was Archibald Roane, Second Governor of Tennessee, 1801-1803.

11. Obituary of Judge John J. Key, *Evening Star*, 13 October 1887.

XII Teapots On the Windowsills

1. *Evening Star*, 22 December 1888, page 11.

2. Ames, Mary Clemmer, *Ten Years in Washington: Life and Scenes in the National Capital as a Woman Sees Them*, Hartford, Conn., pages 370-372.

3. *Evening Star*, 22 December 1888, page 11.

4. Aron, Cindy Sondik, "To Barter Their Souls for Gold," *Journal of American History*, Vol. 67, No. 4, March, 1981, pages 835-853. This essay was awarded the Louis Pelzer Award for 1979. The study was based on a reading of more than 2000 files of female applicants for government jobs. It also contained a statistical analysis of all women applying for clerical jobs in the Treasury Department in 1862-1863. Mrs. Aron is assistant professor of history, specializing in women's history, at the University of Virginia.

5. Ames, *op.cit.*, page 371.

6. Ames, *op.cit.*, page 317.

7. Wadleigh, Frances E., "My Experiences as a Government Clerk," *Lippincott's Magazine*, February 1899, pages 271-279.

8. Wadleigh, *op.cit.*

9. Aron, unpublished dissertation entitled "To Barter Their Souls for Gold," page 231. The prize-winning article cited above represented a distillation of the dissertation.

Georgetown Life, 1865-1900

10. Aron, *op.cit.* page 231
11. *Dictionary of American Biography*, Vol. V, Charles Scribner's Sons, Inc., New York. 1961, page 397.
12. "The Lady of the Treasury," *The Washington Captial*, 12 March 1871, quoted by Aron, page 194 of her dissertation.
13. Aron, dissertation, page 19.
14. Wadleigh, *op. cit.*
15. Aron, dissertation, page 232.

XIII Niederseebach to M Street

1. Manufacturing Schedules, Bureau of the Census, 1880, RG 29, NA.
2. GC, 29 August 1868.
3. Lowenthal, Marvin, *The Jews of Germany*, New York 1964, page 249 ff.
4. Hansen, Marcus Lee, *The Atlantic Migration, 1607-1860*, Harvard University Press, 1930, page 198.
5. Nordlinger, Bernard I., "About My Grandfather Bernard Nordlinger: Confederate Soldier and Unofficial Rabbi," *The Record*. Published by The Jewish Historical Society of Greater Washington, Vol. 3, No. 1, 1968.
6. The 1900 census has a column listing whether a dwelling was rented, owned, or encumbered.
7. Interview with Bernard I. Nordlinger, 23 January 1985.

XIV "An Immense Vessel"

1. Morris, Paul C., *American Sailing Coasters of the North Atlantic*, New York, Bonanza Books, 1979, page 29.
2. *Evening Star*, 2 August 1880.
3. *Ibid.*
4. *Ibid.*
5. Baker, William Avery, *The Maritime History of Bath, Maine and the Kennebec River Region*. Portland, Maine, Anthoeson Press, 1973, Vol. II, pages 567-586.
6. *Evening Star*, 25 August 1880.
7. Baker, *op. cit.*
8. To gauge the dimensions of this trade for Georgetown the years 1884 and 1900 were selected as samples. Every vessel reported in the *Star*'s Georgetown news column as arriving or clearing from its wharves was recorded with its cargo. In each year the arrival of an average one hundred two-, three-, or four-masted schooners was logged. With this count it can be computed that no less than two thousand of these schooners put into and cleared Georgetown Harbor between 1880 and 1900.
9. Most vessels named in the *Star*'s columns were found by name in the *Annual List of Merchant Vessels of the United States* for the years 1884-1901, 30 June 1885, Washington Government Printing Office, 1885. Rig and dimensions are

Notes

listed but not the number of masts. The number often appeared in the *Star*. Another source for this paragraph was Durant, John and Alice, *Pictorial History of American Ships*, A.S. Barnes & Company, New York, 1953, page 233.

10. Insurance maps of the District of Columbia, Vol. 3, New York, Sanborn Map Company, 1888-1903.

11. Parker, Lt. W.J. Lewis, USCG, *The Great Coal Schooners of New England, 1870-1909*, Mystic, Connecticut, The Marine Historical Association, 1948, Vol. II, No. 6, page 63.

12. *Evening Star* (Georgetown Affairs), 8 June 1896; 17 August 1891; 10 January 1898. 1898.

13. In June 1900 the census enumerator cased the riverfront starting at about 35th Street, and found one schooner, probably a two-master, since the ratio was usually two men per mast. He did not list the schooner's name, but all personnel aboard. The data describes a crew typical of that found in most schooners of the era on the Atlantic seabord.

    Capt. - Mgathelin, J. born 1850 Mass. of Mass. parentage
    Mate - Smith, Charles born 1849, Finland, immi. 1871
    2d Mate - Grant, G. born 1877, Georgia.
    Steward - Ohivixon, W. born 1866 Mass.
    Sailor - Syverson, C. born 1868, Norway, immi. 1888.
    " - O'Brien, J. born 1870, Ireland, immi. 1896.
    " - Kisnet, G. born 1863, Germany, immi. 1880.
    " - Nielson, J. born 1862, Sweden, immi. 1880.

Also see Parker *op. cit.*, pages 59-60.

14. *Evening Star*, 9 September 1889.

15. *Ibid.*, 29 June 1910.

XV What's in a Name?

1. GC, 2 January 1872.

2. *Evening Star*, 5 and 31 December 1877.

3. *Ibid.*, 18 November 1880.

4. *Ibid.*, 13 September 1886.

5. Statutes at Large of the United States of America, XXIV, 49th Congress, Sess. I, 1885-1887, page 84.

6. *The Washington Post*, 12 April 1888.

7. *Evening Star*, 22 August 1888.

8. *Ibid.*, 28 August 1899, page 8.

9. Georgetown Tax Assessments, 1875-1878, RG 351, NA.

10. Manufacturing Schedules, Bureau of the Census, 1880, RG 29, NA.

11. *Historical and Commercial Sketches of Washington and Environs, 1884*. Washington, D.C., E.E. Barton, publisher. See G.T. Dunlop article, page 98.

12. Telephone interview with Emily Ecker Bradley, granddaughter of G.T. Dunlop, April 4, 1985.

13. Taggart, Hugh, "Old Georgetown," *Records* of the Columbia Historical Society, Vo. 11, page 21.

Georgetown Life, 1865-1900

XVI Blacks in Residence

1. *Report* of the Health Officer, D.C. Commissioners' *Report*, 1881. Government Printing Office, Washington, D.C., pages 373 ff.
2. The survey is based on the author's findings from the 1900 census.
3. Will of Alfred H. Lee, No. 5705 OS, Office of the Register of Wills, Vol. 13, page 138.
4. Mitchell, Pauline Gaskins, "The History of Mt. Zion United Methodist Church and Mt. Zion Cemetery." *Records* of the Columbia Historical Society, Vol. 51, pp 103-118.
5. *Evening Star*, 27 September 1898.
6. *Ibid.*, 7 October 1873.
7. *Ibid.*, 15 November 1895.
8. *Ibid.*, 22 December 1897.
9. *Ibid.*, 5 June 1897.
10. *Ibid.*, 15 September 1898.
11. Report of the Metropolitan Police, D.C. Comrs. Report, 1892, pages 112-113; page 544; 1895, page 128.
12. *Evening Star*, 8 June 1896; 17 August 1897; 10 January 1898.
13. Green, Constance McLaughlin, *The Secret City*, Princeton, 1967, p. 125.

XVII After-Hours in Georgetown in the 1890s—Part One

1. Stewart, *The Georgetowner*, 21 February 1957.
2. *Evening Star*, 16 April 1884, page 1.
3. *Ibid.*, 25 October 1887, page 6.
4. Ecker, Grace Dunlop, *A Portrait of Old George Town*, page 163.
5. Stewart, *op.cit.*
6. *Evening Star*, 22 December 1888, page 2.
7. Cooke, Maud C., *Social Etiquette* (Springfield, Mass. Hampden Publishing Co., 1896), page 254.
8. *Evening Star*, 17 January 1890, pages 8, 22, 23, 25.
9. *Evening Star*, 24 January 1891, page 11.
10. *Correct Social Usage*, 10th ed. (New York: New York History of Self-Culture, 1902, 1908), 2:464.
11. See Cooke, *Social Etiquette*, page 254.
12. *Evening Star*, 22 December 1888, page 3.
13. For individual data pertaining to the directors, see United States Census 1900, RG 29, NA.
14. See list of leading townsmen who were organizing a Businessmen's Association, *Evening Star*, 27 January 1899, page 8. All lived and worked in Georgetown except Gordon, who only lived there.

Notes

15. See Report on Visit of the Grand Officers of the Grand Lodge of the District to Potomac Lodge No. 5 F.A.A.M., at the Masonic Hall, *Evening Star*, 17 October 1889, page 6.
16. *Evening Star*, 6 June 1897, page 3.
17. *Ibid.*, 29 December 1897, page 9.
18. *Ibid.*, 18 November 1898, page 8.
19. *Ibid.*, 14 May 1888, page 5.
20. *Ibid.*, 26 March 1900, page 12; 29 May 1900, page 5
21. *Christian Endeavor*, 13 November 1898, page 3.
22. Anderson, Jervis, "That was New York: Harlem, Part One of a four-part article, The Journal Uptown," *New Yorker*, 29 June 1981, page 84.
23. Raffe, Walter George, *Dictionary of the Dance* (New York: A.S. Barnes, 1964, 1975), page 84.
24. Washington City *Directories*, 1889-1908.
25. *Evening Star*, October 1896, page 5; 20 April, page 6; 20 August, page 6; 3 August, page 18; 2 November 1897, page 8; 4 January, page 6; 19 May, page 9; 29 June, page 12; 17 November 1898, page 10; 13 April 1899, page 3; 18 August 1900, page 12.
26. *Evening Star*, 30 June 1896, page 51.
27. *Ibid.*, 22 October 1896, page 51.
28. Guest lists for Prof. Schlosser's parties were published after almost every event in the *Evening Star*. Usually the guests were listed as "Misses" or "Messrs" so identifying each one in the city directories was often frustrating. But enough names like Hawkshow, Conlon, Deatdoff, Goebel, with unusual spelling, appeared only once in the column, so it became possible to ascertain their particular address and profession.
29. *Evening Star*, 27 July 1898, page 12.
30. Downey, Fairfax, *Portrait of an Era* as drawn by C.D. Gibson (New York: Charles Scribner & Sons, 1936), page 252.

XVIII   After-Hours in Georgetown in the 1890s—Part Two

1. *Evening Star*, 14 March 1895, page 8; 12 March, page 11; 28 February, page 8; 22 August, 1896, page 5; 22 November, page 10; 29 January, page 5; 19 March 1898, page 8; 25 June, page 8; 18 July 1896, page 11, 23 February 1900, page 7.
2. *Evening Star*, "The Rambler," 13 August pt. 4, page 5; 3 September 1916, pt. 4, page 3; 2 May 1920, pt. 2, page 3.
3. Report of the Harbor-Master, *Report of the Commissioners of the District of Columbia, 1900* (Washington: Government Printing Office, 1900), 1:151.
4. *Evening Star*, 28 April 1900, page 10.
5. *Eminent and Representative Men of Virginia and the District of Columbia in the Nineteenth Century* (Madison, Wisc., Brandt & Fuller, 1893), pp. 333-41.
6. *Evening Star*, 29 April 1899, page 17.
7. Between 24 April 1896, when the Clerk's Assembly, No. 1259, of the Knights

of Labor, met for the first time, and 5 June 1900, this determined group of local small merchants and clerks succeeded in drawing up and signing an agreement, to boycott any merchant closing later than 7 p.m. The Jewish tradesmen were the leaders. The signers were to display in a front window with early-closing, a red triangle with a white border. *Evening Star*, 5 June 1900, page 3.

8. *Evening Star*, 27 December 1898, page 12.
9. *Ibid.*, 31 January 1900, page 11; 1 February 1900, page 14.
10. *Ibid.*, 3 May, page 6; 13 May, page 9, 1898.
11. *Ibid.*, 14 April 1899, page 116.
12. *Ibid.*, 2 December 1897, page 9.
13. *Ibid.*, 22 September 1899, 20 December 1899, page 13.
14. The Act of Congress was passed 23 August 1894. This terminal is described in Le Roy O. King, Jr., *100 Years of Capital Traction* (Washington: Taylor Publishing Co. 1972), page 643.
15. *Ibid.*, page 48.
16. *Evening Star*, "The Rambler," 6 April 1941, page C-6.
17. King, *op. cit.*, page 48.

Bibliography

UNPUBLISHED PRIMARY SOURCES

National Archives hereafter cited as NA:
Records of the District Courts of the United States (21) NA.
Records of the Bureau of the Census 1860, 1870, 1880, 1900 (29) NA.
Records of the Bureau of the Census, Manufacturing Schedules 1880 (29) NA.
Records of the Bureau of Inspection and Navigation (41) NA.
Records of the Internal Revenue Service, Department of the Treasury (58) NA.
Records of the District of Columbia (351) NA.

Records, Oak Hill Cemetery, Georgetown.
Land Records, District of Columbia, 1792-to date.
Magruder, Dr. Hezekiah, Daily Cash Book, 1842-1849. Peabody Collection, Georgetown Public Library.
Reminiscences, typescript, J. Holdsworth Gordon, Peabody Collection.
Renwick-Corcoran Correspondence, Renwick Copybooks, Manuscript Division, LC.
Papers of W.W. Corcoran, Manuscript Division, LC.
Brady, Matthew, Appointment Book, June 1870-December 1875, Division of Prints and Photographs, LC.
Letter from Archibald Roane to the Librarian, Mrs. Parmelee Harrell, 12 August 1876. Tennessee State Library and Archives, Nashville, Tennessee.
Letter from James L. Murphy 16 July 1979, to Mary A. Mitchell.
Pewlist and Communicants Records, St. John's Episcopal Church, 1869-1880.
Street Survey, Peabody Collection.
Aron, Cindy Sondik, "To Barter Their Souls for Gold," unpublished dissertation, History Department, University of Maryland.

PUBLISHED PRIMARY SOURCES

Washington, Alexandria and Georgetown City Directory, 1865-1874. Compiled by William A. Boyd, Washington.
Boyd's Directory of the District of Columbia, (Washington 1875-1900; 1914).
Statutes at Large of the United States, XXIV, 49th Congress, Session I. (Washington, 1885-1887).
Register of Officers and Agents, Civil Military and Naval, in the Service of the United States, 1817-1879, 1879-1922, commonly known as the Official Register (Washington).
Ordinances of the Corporation of Georgetown, 1865-1871.
Reports of the Commissioners of the District of Columbia, 1874-1900. Government Printing Office, Washington.

Georgetown Life, 1865-1900

Report of the Secretary of War, 1866. 49th Congress, 1st Session 1884, Executive Document 138, No. 3 (Washington).

Nordlinger, Bernard I., "About My Grandfather, Bernard Nordlinger: Confederate Soldier and Unofficial Rabbi." *The Record*, Vol. 3, No. 1, 1968, Washington.

Annual List of Merchant Vessels of the United States, 1884-1901 (Washington, 1901).

PICTORIAL

District of Columbia, Washington (City) 1883. Sachse, A. and Company, Geography and Map Division, LC.

Hopkins, G.M., *Real Estate Platbook of Washington, D.C.* (Philadelphia, 1887).

Baist, G. William, Real Estate Atlas of Surveys of Washington, D.C., 1903.

Insurance Maps of the District of Columbia, Vol.3, Sanborn Map company. (New York, 1886, 1903).

NEWSPAPERS

Georgetown Advocate, 1851.
Georgetown Courier, 1866-1876.
Daily National Intelligencer, Washington, 1800-1869.
Daily Constitutional Union, Washington, 1863-1869.
Sunday Morning Chronicle, Washington, 1861-1881.
The Evening Star, Washington, 1852-1981.
The Washington Post, 1877-to date.
The Georgetowner, 1957.

SECONDARY SOURCES

Ames, Mary Clemmer, *Ten Years in Washington: Life and Scenes in the National Capital as a Woman Sees Them.* (Hartford, Conn. 1874).

Aron, Cindy Sondik, "To Barter Their Souls for Gold," *Journal of American History* Vol. 67, No. 4. March 1981.

Austrian, Geoffrey D., *Herman Hollerith: Forgotten Giant of Information Processing.* (New York, 1982).

Baker, William Avery, *The Maritime History of Bath, Maine and the Kennebec River Region.* (Portland, Maine, 1973).

Cohen, Henry, *The Career Biography of W.W. Corcoran.* (Westport, Conn. 1971). This book is No. 4 in a series called *Business and Politics from Age of Jackson to the Civil War*.

Columbia Historical Society *Records*, Vols. 1-51. Washington, D.C.

Correct Social Usage, (New York, 1908).

Cross, Marian E. *Pioneer Harvest* (Minneapolis, 1949).

Eminent and Representative Men of Virginia and the District of Columbia in the Nineteenth Century (Madison, Wis. 1893).

Bibiography

Cooke, Ward C., *Social Etiquette* (Springfield, Mass. 1896).
Dictionary of American Biography, 22 Vols. (New York, 1915).
Downey, Fairfax, *Portrait of an Era* (New York, 1936).
Ecker, Grace Dunlop, *Portrait of Old Georgetown* (Richmond, 1951).
Garrison, Fielder H., *John Shaw Billings* (New York, 1915).
Green, Constance McLaughlin, *The Secret City* (Princeton, 1967). *Washington: A History of the Capital, 1800-1950* (Princeton, 1962).
Gutheim, Frederick, *The Potomac* (New York, 1949).
Hansen, Marcus Lee, *The Atlantic Emigration 1607-1860* (Cambridge, Mass., 1930).
Historical and Commercial Sketches of Washington and Environs (Washington, 1884).
Holt, Emily, *Encyclopedia of Etiquette* (New York, 1916).
King, LeRoy O., Jr., *100 Years of Capital Traction* (Washington, 1972).
Lowenthal, Marvin, *The Jews of Germany* (Washington, 1972).
Morris, Paul C. *American Sailing Coasters of the North Atlantic* (New York, 1979).
Mitchell, Mary, *Divided Town* (Barre 1968).
Morgan, Maxine Goff, *A Chronological History of the Alexandria Canal*, (Arlington, Va. 1966).
Oberholzer, E.P., *Jay Cooke, Financier of the Union Army* (Franklin, N.Y. 1907).
Parker, Lt. W.J. Lewis, USCG, *The Great Coal Schooners of New England, 1870-1909*. (Mystic, Conn. 1948).
The Presbyterian Congregation in Georgetown, 1780-1970. Published by a Session of the Presbyterian Congregation in Georgetown, Washington, D.C., 1971.
Proctor, John Clagett, *Washington Past and Present* Vols. I-V (Washington, 1930).
Sanderlin, Walter S., *The Great National Project: A History of the Chesapeake & Ohio Canal*. Johns Hopkins University Studies in Historical and Political Science, LXIV, No. 1, (Baltimore, 1946).
U.S. Civil Service Comission, *The Biography of an Ideal*, (Washington, 1974).
Whyte, James H., *The Uncivil War* (New York, 1958).

Acknowledgments

Research for this book started with making my own copy of the 1880 census, the original of which was available at the Columbia Historical Society. The Heurich Building, owned and occupied by the Society, was convenient to reach by bus, and Perry G. Fisher, then executive director, kindly cleared out a large space for me on the third floor in the sunny, secluded tower. Almost immediately names familiar to me from my Civil War research showed up, and Mr. Fisher gave invaluable assistance in locating material about these individuals in the Society's abundant archives. Among the documents he uncovered was a salary and grade schedule for federal clerks, which he found in some Georgetown Customhouse records. Later, when I was working in the Treasury library, even the librarian there was unable to find such a chart. Perry would send me copies of clippings or photographs whenever he thought they were relevant. Betsy Miller, then curator, did the same thing. I am grateful to both for keeping my needs in mind during their own distracting and demanding schedules at the Society.

The next initiative was lengthy and meaty, and continued right to the end of this book. This was reading the *Evening Star*'s Georgetown news column which appeared almost daily during the last decades of the nineteenth century. Here is where Rosilla Hawes came into the picture as a most able volunteer researcher. With amazing zeal and a sharp eye for scandal, crime, and other human interest material, she plowed through issue after issue gathering colorful data. For almost three years, on and off, she also helped with the tedious task of tracing individual newcomers and foreigners through city directories to find out how long they lived in Georgetown and how many addresses they had occupied. She hunted up obituaries. She kept a file on Red Bill's frenetic activity. She built up the picture of the Georgetown Assembly and its members. I am thankful for the time, energy and good will she expended for what sometimes seemed to us both a long-shot goal. When and how all this good material would get pulled together and see printer's ink was a question we occasionally discussed.

At length the research led me into the Nineties, and another helper joined the effort. A professional researcher, Hazel Kreinheder showed unflagging energy and imagination in developing the scenario of the waterfront between 1880 and 1910 when three- and four-masted schooners moved in and out of the harbor with their cargoes of ice and coal. During the Eighties and Nineties many new houses went up in Georgetown, and finding building permits for each was the only accurate way to date them. Hazel found scores of them, by knowing her way around the National Archives' search-rooms. Reading the daily *Evening Star* 1895-1900, she amassed data that was invaluable in describing the two separate worlds of turn-of-the-century Georgetown, the one white, the other black. Her tenacity and acumen brought me invaluable help.

Four of the Chronicles were written for specific purposes. The piece about William W. Corcoran and Oak Hill Cemetery was read before the Columbia Historical Society in 1979. A second, "An Immense Vessel," was read at the Annual Conference on Washington History organized by the Columbia Historical Society and the George Washington University History department. A third, "Teapots on the Windowsills," was read at a meeting of the Evermay Club whose thirty members gather in Georgetown seven times a year to hear a member read an original paper on a certain theme. In my year the theme was "Invasion," and I described the invasion of the first women clerks into the Treasury Department. To the program chairman of each of these groups I am profoundly grateful for the chance and incentive to assemble my material, write it up, and then read it before a knowledgeable audience.

The fourth incentive came from J. Kirkpatrick Flack, editor of the Columbia Historical Society *Records*, who gave me a boost when he wanted to print "After-Hours in the 1890s" in the 51st volume. I am grateful to him also for his thoughtful and thorough editing of the piece and for permission to reprint it in this volume.

Associate Professor Ronald M. Johnson, of Georgetown University's History Department, was kind enough to read my draft of "Blacks in Residence," and to give it a thoughtful critique and encouraging suggestions about how to develop the material further.

Some rich background came from two men who had grown up in Georgetown. Dr. Henry G. Wagner told me about his grandfather and namesake who built the *Ludlow Patton*; Bernard Nordlinger pulled out family archives about his grandfather, the immigrant from France in the antebellum era.

Credit should be given to Agnes Mullins for her deliberation in identifying the site of Arlington House in the print of the *Ludlow Patton*; and also to Sarah Collins, archivist at the Arlington County Library, Central Branch, who researched the history of the Ross Farm and its appearance in the Civil War era.

Additional background and assistance came from Eleanor Cropley and Virginia Hollerith, both of whom grew up in Georgetown and had colorful stories to tell.

My most frequent place of research was the Washingtoniana Room of the Martin Luther King Library. Here I heard G. R. F. Key, a reference librarian, describe his growing-up years on Thomas Jefferson Street. Kathryn Ray was always generous with her thorough knowledge of the Room's collections and her time. On one occasion Mary Ternes found an important clipping in the massive *Star* collection I would never have found on my own. All in all, a wonderful place to work, beautifully organized and staffed with fine librarians.

Finally, I give my warmest thanks to Dave Roffman, editor and publisher of *The Georgetowner*, our splendid local newspaper, and Chandler Hottel, business manager, for their cooperation in printing my first text, chapter by chapter, between October 1984 and July 1985. Here again, the incentive to write up the material into a cohesive, literate whole was useful in producing what eventually became the manuscript for this book.

Index

A

Accidents reported in newspaper, 4-5, 43, 44, 87
Acker, Nicholas, stonemason, 33
Adams Express Office, 54
The Alaska (Canalboat), 57
Alexandria Canal Company, 4
Alexandria Holding Company, 85
Alexandria, retrocession to Virginia, 53
Altair Cycle Club, 104
American Dredging Company, 12
American Ice Company, 81
Analostan (Roosevelt) Island, 14, 78, 104
Ancient Daughters of Tabitha, 91
Animal control, 3, 26
Aqueduct Bridge, 3-4, 57-58, 85-86, 89; *illus.*, 56, 85
Architecture, 23, 52
Arlington Hotel, 12
Arlington House. *See* Custis-Lee Mansion.
Art collections, 105
Assembly Club. *See* Georgetown Assembly.
Atlantic Coast Seamen's Union, 82

B

Bachellor's German, 96-97
Back Street. *See* Q Street.
Baer, Benoit, clothier, 76
Baker, Newton D., Mrs., 19
Balch, Stephen Bloomer, 45
Baltimore & Ohio Railroad, 11, 54, 83
Bank of Columbia, 14
Barber, Mrs. Margaret, 20
Barbershops, 14
Barker, Daniel, Oak Hill Cemetery superintendent, 41
Bartholdi (Steamer), 104
Baseball clubs, 104; *illus.*, 103
Beall, Emily, 97
Beall, George W., 37
Beall, Ninian, Rock of Dumbarton, 42
Beall Street, 84
Beall, Thomas, of George, 30, 98
Bell, Alexander Graham, 64
Bell, Alexander Melville, 63-64; house *illus.*, 62
Bell, David, 63
Bicycling, 102, 107-109; *illus.*, 101
Billings, Caroline, 61
Billings, John Shaw, 44, 61-62, 97
Birch's Funeral Establishment, 86
Black Code, 6, 8
Blacks
  businessmen, 91
  church congregations of, 91
  housing, 45, 48, 90
  occupations, 9, 12
  lodge members, 91
  political activity of, 6
  population of
    (1860) free Negroes, 8
    (1864) estimates, 8

Index

(1867) census, 9
(1870) census, 10
(1872-74), color not designated, 9
(1879) health survey, 90
(1885) police reports, 90
(1900) status, 90-94
shrinking population of, 92
refugees, 7, 10
separate but equal legislation, 94
Blundon, John A., Oak Hill Cemetery superintendent, 31-32, 35-36, 38
Board of Public Works, xii, 5, 25-26, 42
Bodisco house, 49, 110
Boggs, Mrs. Ellen, 45
Boggs, William Brenton, 45
Borden's Wharf, 78
"Boston" (red light district), 82, 93
Brady, Matthew, porcelain head of Guy Cooke crafted by, 26
Brewer, Henry, surveyor, 37
Bridge Street
128 Bridge Street, 4
Bridge Street Presbyterian Church, 45
Bright's Disease, 26, 28
"Brinetown," 92
Broome, Isaac, sculptor, 33-34
Brown, Robert I., Company. See Robert I. Brown Company.
Buckey & Marbury's Hardware Store, 43
Building associations, 53, 60
Burleith, 48

"Buzzard's Roost". See Foxall mansion.

C

C. I. B. club, 104
C & O Canal. See Chesapeake & Ohio Canal.
Cabin John Bridge (Union Arch), 108
Cabin John Hotel, 108
Cakewalk, 99
Canalboats, naming of, 57
Capital Traction Company, 88-89, 92, 107
The Carriage House, 72
Casilear, George, engraver, 62-63
Catholics, Roman, interest in art, 105
Chain Bridge, 3, 8, 59, 98
Chase Salmon P.
burial site, 18
friendship with Henry D. Cooke, 18, 27
hiring of women, 65
Chautauqua Association, 108
Chesapeake & Ohio Canal, 11, 107
See also Ludlow Patton
Chesapeake & Ohio Canal Company
The Mole, 81
scrip for wages, 77
Children's Hospital, 98
Christ Episcopal Church, 1, 20, 95

132

Church, Charles B., 79, 81
The City of Washington: An Illustrated History, 57
Clerks. *See* Federal clerks.
Coal trade, 2, 4, 12, 55, 57-58, 79, 80-82, 87; *illus.*, 80
Collins, Joseph F., contractor, 20
Colt (Ship), 14
Columbia Lodge, 91
Conduit Road (MacArthur Boulevard), 92
Connecticut Pie Company, 72-73, 86; *illus.*, 73
Cooke, Eleutheros, 17
  portrait of, 18, 21
Cooke, Guy, death of, 26
Cooke, Henry David, 17-28
  burial site, 17
  charter repeal supporter, 11
  death of, 28
  disease control, 2-3
  District of Columbia Governor, 17
  executor, will, Salmon P. Chase, 27
  Georgetown Amateur Orchestra organizer, 104
  health of, 26, 28
  mansion, 98; *illus.*, 19
  portrait of, *illus.*, 18
  railroad development, 88
  receptions, 27
Cooke, Henry David, Jr., wedding, 27
Cooke, Laura, 17
Cooke, Lizzie, death of, 23
Cooke Park, 98

Cooke, Pitt, 97
Cooke Row, 15, 21-23, 98; *illus.*, 25
Copperthite, Henry, baker, 72-73
Corcoran Gallery of Art, first official meeting of the board, 24
Corcoran, James M., 41
Corcoran, Louise, 35
Corcoran, Louise Morris, death of, 29
Corcoran & Riggs Bank, 29, 35
Corcoran, William Wilson
  Arlington Hotel builder, 12
  charter repeal supporter, 11
  library trustee, 48
  Oak Hill Cemetery benefactor, 29
  portrait of, *illus.*, 30
  See also Oak Hill Cemetery.
Cox, Richard S., estate, 48
Cox Row, 109-110
Cox, Walter S., Oak Hill Cemetery secretary-treasurer, 31
Cox's Tannery, 90
Coyle, Randolph, surveyor, 40
Cumberland, Maryland. *See* Coal trade. *See also Ludlow Patton*
Curtis School, 48, 92
Custis, George Washington Parke, 59
Custis-Lee Mansion, 59
Cycle Clubhouse, 92

Index

D

Dancing schools, 99-102
Darne, R. H., 93
Darneille, Philip H., realtor, 51, 96, 97
Davis, Jefferson, 108
  burial site of son, 34
de la Roche, George, Oak Hill Cemetery architect, 30, 37
Deeble, James W., Oak Hill Cemetery secretary-treasurer, 32, 38, 41
Dickson, John, house, 10
Disease control
  diptheria and yellow fever epidemics, 54
  horse disease epidemic, 43
  lack of, 2-3
Dodge, A. H., 27
Dodge, Anna Howell, wedding, 27
Dodge, Charles, 36
Dodge, Elizabeth, 36
Dodge, Emily, 50
Dodge farm, 50
Dodge, Francis, Jr., 19
Dore, Gustave, illustrator, 20-21
Downing, Andrew Jackson, architect, 20, 31
Downing & Vaux House, 17
Drovers Rest Cattle Market, 3, 26
Drug stores, 13-14
Dumbarton Avenue, 45
  2732 Dumbarton Avenue, 92
  3035 Dumbarton Avenue, 45
  3127 Dumbarton Avenue, *illus.*, 49
Dumbarton Club, 99
Dumbarton Methodist Episcopal Church, 1
Dumbarton Oaks. *See* The Oaks.
Dunlop, George Thomas, 88-89; *illus.*, 88
Duvall Foundry, 55

E

E. C. Knight (Steamer), 12
Eastern Star, Order of the, 107
Ebenezer A. M. E. Church, 6, 92
Edgewood, estate sale, 27-28
Education, 10
Eliza (Schooner), 33
Employment. *See* Blacks; Men in federal service; Occupations; Women in federal service.
English's, Miss, Seminary, 10
Epidemics. *See* Disease control.
Epworth League, Embury Chapter, 91
Eustis, George, Jr., 35
Evermay estate, 36

F

F. & A. H. Dodge, 19
Farmers & Mechanics Bank, 32, 48, 75, 87
Federal clerks, 60-71; numbers of, 60, 65

Ferguson, John, barber, 92
Fertilizer industry, 88
Fifteenth Street
   452 15th Street, 18
Fire prevention, 5, 13
First National Bank of Washington, 18
Forrest, Bladen, 95
Forrest family home, 110
Forrest Hall, 14, 95
Fourteenth Street Bridge. *See* Long Bridge.
Foxall Foundry, 57, 86
Foxall, Henry, mansion, 82; *illus.*, 93
Frederick Street, 84
Frisby, Edgar, scientist, 14
Fritch, George, 73-74
Frog Island. *See* "Boston".

G

Gale, Dennis, 110
Gay Street, 84
General Land Office, 65
Georgetown
   charter of 1751, 11, 25
   commercial life of
     See M Street; Waterfront; Wisconsin Avenue
   name controversy, 84-85
   name officially abolished in 1895, 89
   population of
     (1880), 109
     (1885), 90
     (1900), 109
   retrocession to Maryland, 11-12, 53-54
   recreational advantages of, 13-14, 19, 60-61, 64, 72, 98-99, 103-104, 106-108
   relationship to federal government
     appointment of commissioners as governing body (1874), 47
     charter (1751), 11, 25
     name abolished by Act of Congress (1895), 89
     Organic Act (1878), 54
     retrocession to Maryland considered, 11-12, 53-54
     tax assessments slashed, 53-54
     Territorial Act (1871), 25-26
     threat to abolish its name, 84
   social advantages of, 61, 95
   terminus for street railways
     Georgetown & Tenallytown Railroad, 86
     Washington & Georgetown Railroad, 18, 88
     Washington & Great Falls Railroad, 89
     Washington, Arlington & Falls Church Railway, 89
     See also Capital Traction Company
Georgetown Amateur Orchestra, 104-105
Georgetown Assembly, 89, 95-102
Georgetown Corporation
   Lincoln, Abraham, reaction to assassination of, 1

Index

Negro Suffrage Bill, opposition to, 6
notes redeemed, 26
Georgetown Courier (1865-1876), 4
Georgetown Hospital, 94
Georgetown Improvement Company, 50-51
Georgetown Patriarchs, 91
Georgetown Seminary, 10
Georgetown University, 89, 92
Georgetown-Tenallytown Railroad, 86-87; *illus.*, 87
German (Cotillion). *See* Bachellor's German.
Gibson, Charles Dana, 101
Gibson Girl, 100-102; with her beau, *illus.*, 100
Gilbert, Henry P., 51
Glen Echo amphitheatre, 108
Glymont, riverside resort, 14, 24, 104
Good Samaritan Church, 91
Gordon, J. Holdsworth, 98-99
Gordon, William A., 98
Grace Church, 28
Grand United Order of Odd Fellows (G.U.O.O.F.), 91-92
Grant, Ulysses S., reception at Cooke house, *illus.*, 24
Grant-Colfax club, 6
Graves, Emma R., 68-69
Gwin, William M., 34

H

H Street
  1611 H Street, 32
Hall, Asaph, astronomer, 62; *illus.*, 63
Harewood, Corcoran country estate, 3
Hawthorne Social Club, 92
The Heights, 2
  See also Oak Hill Cemetery.
Heliotrope Circle, 92
"Henry Addison" (Fire steamer), 5, 13
Herr, Abraham, 49-50
Herring Hill, 8, 42, 45, 90
Hickory Nut Hill, 48
High Service Reservoir, 51
Hill, George, papermill owner, 41
Hollerith, Herman, 61-62; *illus.*, 64, tabulating card, 62
Hollerith, Virginia, 61
Holy Trinity Church, 44, 47
Holyrood Cemetery, 91
Home for the Blind, 51
Hot Foot Club, 104
Housing
  construction from 1860 to 1870, 15
  construction of single-family homes, 109
  dwelling count (1876), 52
  ratings for 1879 health survey, 90
Hungary Hill. *See* "Boston".
Hunter, Robert, 50
Hutchinson, Abby, 57
Hyde, Anthony, 35, 37

I

Ice trade, 79-80, 105
Immigrants. *See* Refugees.
Independent Ice Company, 79-80
Independent Order of Odd
   Fellows, 106
International Athletic Club, 107
International Seamen's Union, 82
Irish community, 46, 92

J

Jacob's Park (Rose Park), 6, 92
Jay Cooke & Co., 17-18, 27
Jewish community, 74-77
Johns Hopkins Hospital, 61
Jones, Fred W., 41
Joyce, Mrs. John, 68-69

K

Kaiser, K., frescoes, 20
Kengla family, 48
Kennebec Ice Company, 54
Kennebec River ice, 58, 78, 80
Kesher Israel Congregation, 77
Key, Judge John J., 63
King, Henry, Oak Hill Cemetery
   secretary-treasurer, 31-32
King, Preston, 69
King, William H., Oak Hill
   Cemetery accountant, 38
Knights of St. John, 91
Knights Templar of the Potomac
   Commandery No. 3, 106

L

Ladies' German Club, 96
Lafayette Square Opera House, 105
Laird, William, Jr., 97
Lambden, Carolyn, 59
Land values, 54
Lang's Hotel, 9
Lee, Alfred, 91
Lee, Aloysius, 91
Lee, George Washington Custis, 59
Lee, John T., 91
Lee, Robert E., 38
Lee, Robert E., Mrs., 59
Lee, W. H. F., 86
Lee, William H., 91
Legal Tender Act, 65
Libbey, J. Edward, 50
Libbey, Joseph, 50, 98
Library. *See* Peabody Library.
Lincoln, Abraham, assassination, 1
Linthicum, Edward, 2
Linthicum family, 47
Linthicum Hall, 96, 99-100
Linthicum Institute, 14, 95
Lipscomb, Miss Sallie A., boarding
   and day school, 10, 51
The Little Red House, 69
Livery-stables, 21
Long Bridge (14th Street Bridge),
   3, 58, 85

Index

Louisa Moore (Ship), 12
Ludlow Patton (Steam canal barge), 55-59; *illus.*, 56
Lyons' Mill bridge, 1

M

M Street, 74
    2904 to 2906 M Street, 91
    3007 M Street, 100
    3103 M Street, 76
    3127 M Street, 4
    3128 M Street, 76
    3130 M Street, 76
    3200 M Street, 88
    3221 M Street, 55
    3285 M Street, 42
    Board of Public Works improvements, 42-43
MacArthur Boulevard. *See* Chain Bridge Road.
Mackall, Leonard, family, 92
Magruder, Hezekiah, 46
Marbury, John, Oak Hill Cemetery president, 31, 35, 38
Marbury, Mrs. Mary, 19
Mary Washington (Steamer), 104
Masonic orders, 106-107
Matthews, Charles M., Oak Hill Cemetery president, 41
Matthews, Emily C., 99
McCullough, Andrew, 67
McGill, John D., editor of *Georgetown Courier*, 4-5, 53, 84

Medical practice, 5
Men in federal service, 60-64
Merrick, R. T., Judge Advocate, 41
Methodist Cemetery, 8
Metropolitan Electric Railroad, 100
Metropolitan Rail Road, 48
Mill Street
    Oak Hill Cemetery wall, 37-38
Minerva Club, 14
Minerva House of Ruth, 91
Mite Missionary Society, 91
The Mole, 81
Monroe (or 27th) Street, 45
Moore, F. L., Agricultural Company, *illus.*, 87
Morris, Charles, 34
Morsell House, 10
Morsell, Judge, 51
Mount Alto. *See* Red Hill.
Mount Hope, 99
Mount Zion United Methodist Church, 8, 10, 91-92
Murphy, Edgar, 91
Music, 104-105

N

N Street
    2715 N Street, 62
    2801 N Street, 77
    3017 N Street, 10, 19
    3019 N Street, 62
    3025 N Street, 44
    3027 N Street, 44, 61

3032 N Street, 77
3038 N Street, 44
3113 N Street, 76-77
3265 N Street, 44
3337 N Street, 97
3339 N Street, 110
National Bank of Washington, Georgetown Branch, 43
Negro suffrage, 6, 14; at the ballot box, *illus.*, 7
Negro Suffrage Bill, 6
New Cut Road, improvements, 3
Nordlinger, Bernard, 75-77; *illus.*, 76
Nordlinger, Bernard I., 76
Nordlinger, Hannah, 76
Nordlinger, Isaac B., 76
Nordlinger, Isaac W., 77
Nordlinger, Wolf, clothier, 75-77
Norfolk, boating trips from Georgetown, 14

O. D. Witherill (Schooner), 58
O Street
   3016 O Street, 23
   3121 O Street, *illus.*, 52
   3300 O Street, 105
   3314 O Street, 49, 52
   3318 O Street, 49-50, 52
   3322 O Street, 49-50; *illus.*, 50
   3328 O Street, 50
   3331 O Street, 50
   See also Curtis School; Ebenezer Church; Linthicum Institute; St. John's Episcopal Church.
Oak Hill Cemetery, 17-18, 29-41, 45, 61
   burial site of: Bodisco, Alexandre de, Baron, 49; Chase Salmon P., 18; Cooke, Henry David, 17
   Corcoran family vault, 32-34
Oak Hill Chapel
   designed by James W. Renwick, Jr., 31, 32
   memorial service for Henry David Cooke, 28
The Oaks (Dumbarton Oaks), 2
Occupations
   for black community, 8
   for refugees, 9
   for women, 66
   See also Men in federal service; Women in federal service.
O'Donnell's Drug Store, 87
Offley, Holmes, 50
Ohio State Journal, 17-18
Old Syc, 44
Olive Street, bottling factory, 2, 13, 74
O'Neall, Ann, 14
Orchestra. *See* Georgetown Amateur Orchestra.
Organic Act of 1878, 54

Index

P

P Street
  2819 P Street, 27
  3043 P Street, 50, 98
  3052 P Street, 19
  3053 P Street, 50
  3100 P Street, 51
  3108 P Street, 10
  3315 P Street, 46
  3327 P Street, 63
Palmer's Bottling Depot, 90
Papermill Bridge, 1
Paradise Flats. *See* "Boston".
Paradise Lost, 20, 27
Passeno boathouse, 47
Patton, Ludlow, 57
  See also Ludlow Patton (Steam canal barge).
Peabody, George, 36
Peabody Library, 48
Peck family, 47
Pendleton Act, 61
Peter, Martha Parke Custis, 22, 51
Philippine Islands independence, 106
Pickrell, Esau, 49
Pickrell house, 50
Pickrell, Virginia (Mrs. Esau), 49
Pickrell warehouse, 47
Plowman, Thomas B., architect, 20
"Pocket Tuileries." *See* Union Hotel.
Poe mansion, 14
Police stationhouse, 12
Pope, Alfred, 91
Population
  (1880 to 1900), 109
  (1900), householders, 110
  (1901), heads of household, 64
  See also Blacks
Port of Entry, Georgetown, xxi
Post Office
  abolished in Georgetown, 84
  block, 51-52
Potomac Boat Club, 104
Potomac Electric Power Company, 109
Potomac Insurance Company, 31
Potomac Lodge No. 5, 98, 106
Potomac Street, 93
Potomac Union Lodge, 91
Presbyterian Cemetery, 8, 45, 73
Presbyterian Church, 51
Progressive League, 91
Progressive Republican clubs, 6
Prospect Avenue
  3309 Prospect Avenue, 37
  3508 Prospect Avenue, 63
Poe mansion, 14

Q

Q Street
  1868 to 1873 Q Street, 15
  2900 Q Street, 10
  3007 Q Street, 27
  3019 Q Street, 27
  3021 Q Street, 98
  3102 Q Street, 88

building of Cooke Row, 23
opening of, 22

R

R Street, 51
   2920 R Street, 30
   3238 R Street, 69
   Mount Hope, 99
   Oak Hill Cemetery gates, 29
   See also Road Street.
Railroad development, 4, 45, 107-108
Red Bill and his gang, 82, 93
Red Hill (Mount Alto), 24
"Red Hot" (firehorse), 5, 13
Refugees, 9, 48, 74-85
Reno Hill, 17
Renwick Gallery, 35
Renwick, James, Jr.
   Oak Hill Chapel architect, 31, 32
   Webster, Daniel, house renovation, 32
Reservoir Road. See New Cut Road.
"Restoration in Georgetown, 1915-1965," 110
Retrocession. See Alexandria; Georgetown.
Riggs, Elisha, library trustee, 48
Riggs, George W., 11
Rittenhouse, David, 99
Road Street, 30, 47
Roane, Archibald, 63

Robert I. Brown Company, 32-33
Rock Creek
   baptisms in, 6
   barrier between Georgetown and Washington, 7, 48
   boundary, Oak Hill Cemetery, 19
   bridge over, at P Street, 1, 24
   dump created near, 45
   east terminus, M Street, 86
   obstacle, Hares and Hounds, 98
   site of black housing in 1880s, 90
   site of C&O Canal Company's Mole, 81
   site of Corcoran monument, 30
   U.S. Naval Observatory, 60
Rock of Dumbarton, 30, 42
Rockville Pike, 11
Rod and Gun Club, 104
Roosevelt Island. See Analostan Island.
Rose Park. See Jacob's Park.
Ross, William Henry, 58-59
Rosslyn, derivation of name, 59
Rosslyn Development Corporation, 59

S

Saloons, 86, 93
Sanger, William P. S., 36-38, 50
Schladt, Joseph, 72
Schlosser, Henry, dancing teacher, 99-102

Index

Scott, Douglas Gordon, 49
Scott, Harriett Beall (Williams), death of, 50
Searle, Henry E., architect, 13
The Secret City, 9
Segregation legalized, 94
Seminary Hotel (now Colonial Apartments), 9, 95
Shekell, A. B., 92
Shepherd, Alexander R., 24, 25, 38, 42
Shinn, Riley A.
  bottling factory on Olive Street, 2, 13, 74
  quoted on Georgetown development, 52
  Union Hotel builder, 13, 42
Shoemaker, George, 52
Shoemaker, William, poet, 4
Sisters of Mary, 91
Slums, 110
Smackum family, 8
Smallwood family, 8
Smith, Boyd, 49
Smith Row, 44
Smithsonian Institution, 61
Southworth, Emma E.D.N., writer, 4
Spanish-American War, 105, 107
Spinner, Francis, 65
Spofford, Ainsworth, 48
St. John's Episcopal Church, 8, 20
  baptismal font, 26
  funeral for Henry David Cooke, 28
St. Mary's Guild, Ladies of Virginia, 98

Starkweather & Plowman, 23, 38
Steele, Franklin, realtor, 63
Stevens, Oscar, 44
Stohlmann's Ice Cream parlor, 104

T

Talcott, Lucia, 62
Taverns
  Drovers Rest Cattle Market, 3
  John Orme tavern, *illus.*, 87
  O and Wisconsin Avenue, 6
Tenallytown Road, 11, 47-48
Tenney, William H., quote on survival of the bobtail bull, 11
Territorial Act of 1871, 1, 25-26
Thian, Raphael Principe, 63
Thirtieth Street
  1517 30th Street; 18-21; *illus.*, 19, 21
  1537 30th Street, 17
Thirty-fifth Street
  1525 35th Street, 14; *illus.*, 62
Thiry-first Street
  1054 31st Street (now Canal Square shopping mall), 62
  1517 31st Street, 98
  1627 31st Street, 51, 96
Thirty-fourth Street
  Foxall mansion, 82; *illus.*, 93
Thirty-third Street
  1418-1426 33rd Street, 49
  1507 33rd Street, 73-74
  Cemetery, 45

Index

Thomas, Lorenzo, Oak Hill Cemetery treasurer, 31
Three Sisters Rocks, 59
Tournaments on Analostan Island, 14
Townsend, George Allen, poem by, 69
Train, Charles Russell, with baseball squad, *illus.*, 103
Treasury, employment of women, 65-68
Trolley cars. *See* Railroad development.
Tudor Place, 22, 51
Tudor Place Lawn Tennis Club, 98
Twenty-eighth Street
  1403 28th Street, 92
Twenty-ninth Street
  1334 29th Street, 91
  1617 29th Street, 61

U

Union Arch. *See* Cabin John Bridge.
Union Hospital, 10
Union Hotel, 9, 13, 42, 95; *illus.*, 13
United States Chamber of Commerce, 32
United States Gazette, 17
United States Naval Observatory, 20, 60

V

Vaux, Calvert, 20
Velocipede Riding School, 15
Visitation Academy, 44
Volta Place
  3301 Volta Place, *illus.*, 74
  3322 Volta Place, 73

W

Wadleigh, Frances E., clerk, 68
Waggaman, Charlotte, 105
Waggaman, Thomas E., real estate broker, 105
Wagner, Henry G., inventor and clockmaker, 55, 57, 59
Walter, Thomas U., architect, 32-33
Washington, Arlington & Falls Church Railway, 89
Washington, George Corbin, 30
Washington & Georgetown Railroad, 18, 88
Washington & Great Falls Railroad, 89
Washington, Martha, 59
Waterfront
  coal shipping on, 12
  end of, as commercial focus, 82-83
  Irish labor on, 92
  manufacturing on, 12
  real estate values lowered on, 53
  revival as a port, 79-82

Index

terminal, Georgetown & Tenallytown Railroad, 87
transportation routes improved, 47
Wawaset (Steamer), 14
Weaver family, 48
Weaver's Hardware Store, 100, 106
Webster, Daniel, house, 32
Welch, Charles D., 6
West Georgetown Methodist Church, 10
West Washington, nee Georgetown, 84-85
Western High School, 92
Wheatley, Walter, 99

"The White Cow" *See* Bank of Columbia.
Widows, 109
Widows' Lodge, 91
William L. White (Schooner), 78-79; *illus.*, 78
Williams, Brooke, 51
Williams, Harriet Beall, 49
Williams, Rebecca, 51
Wisconsin Avenue, 72
   1216 Wisconsin Avenue, 72
   1264 Wisconsin Avenue, 95
Women
   in federal service, 65-71
   new independence of, 70
   social freedom of, 101, 107

About the author

"Georgetown's biographer," Mary Mitchell, once again catches the distinctive flavor of her adopted community in this volume about life in Georgetown during the latter part of the 19th century. A Minnesotan by birth, Mitchell moved to Washington in 1953 and to Georgetown in 1981. Since 1959 she has immersed herself in its public records and archives, its newspaper files and documents, to dig out the wealth of little known historical episodes which this book brings to life. Without neglecting the major economic and political factors shaping Georgetown's past and present, she keeps her eye on events of color and human interest. Her previous Georgetown books have included two photographic essays, *A Walk In Georgetown* and *Glimpses of Georgetown*, and a study about the community during the Civil War, *Divided Town*.